ROCK
RECONSIDERED

Steve Lawhead

A Christian Looks at Contemporary Music

InterVarsity Press
Downers Grove
Illinois 60515

InterVarsity Press is the book-publishing division of Inter-Varsity Christian Fellowship, a student movement active on campus at hundreds of universities, colleges and schools of nursing. For information about local and regional activities, write IVCF, 233 Langdon St., Madison, WI 53703.

Distributed in Canada through InterVarsity Press, 1875 Leslie St., Unit 10, Don Mills, Ontario M3B 2M5, Canada.

ISBN 0-87784-812-2

Printed in the United States of America

Library of Congress Cataloging in Publication Data

Lawhead, Steve
　　Rock reconsidered.

　　Bibliography: p.
　　1. Rock music–History and criticism.　2. Music and morals.　I. Title.
ML3534.L39　　　　261.5'7　　　81-8129
ISBN 0-87784-812-2　　　　AACR2

| 17 | 16 | 15 | 14 | 13 | 12 | 11 | 10 | 9 | 8 | 7 | 6 | 5 | 4 | 3 | 2 | 1 |
| 95 | 94 | 93 | 92 | 91 | 90 | 89 | 88 | 87 | 86 | 85 | 84 | 83 | 82 | 81 |

*To Alice and Ross
and to my parents Robert and Lois,
for their steadfast support
and enduring encouragement.*

Acknowledgments
*This book is the work
of much time and many hands. I am
indebted to these who
have so generously shared their
time and talents: Alice
Lawhead, Philip Yancey,
Harold Smith, Jim Long and all
those who read this
manuscript as it developed and
whose criticisms have
helped to make it stronger.*

PART I

THE ROOTS OF ROCK

1

FIRE IS THE
DEVIL'S ONLY FRIEND

A GROUP OF THIRTY ASSORTED young people and a handful of adults are standing casually around a large metal tub. The tub is placed exactly in the center of a church parking lot. The last light of day is fading; and as the shadows stretch across the asphalt a tingle of excitement grows, a thrill of repressed high spirits.

One by one others are added to the number. Each one brings a sacrifice: an armful of flat, cardboard envelopes containing rock 'n' roll records. These are thrown into the tub with the rest. The pyramid-shaped pile continues to grow.

Someone arrives with a guitar and begins to strum a chorus. A few voices join in, and soon most are singing. The night air holds a slight chill now that it is almost dark.

It is time for the ceremony to begin. The leader steps forward, producing a can of charcoal lighting fluid which he squeezes liberally over the stack of assorted albums, tapes, books and T-shirts in the large metal tub. Now the group falls silent. Expectant.

The man begins to speak, and when he has finished he strikes a match which sputters in the dark, the tiny flare glittering in the reflection of dozens of wide, watching eyes. The group crowds closer around the tub.

The match falls. A flame licks out, climbs the side of the pyramid. A finger of flame races around the inner rim of the tub, igniting the contents. And then, with an audible whoosh! the pyre shimmers in a dancing curtain of fire. The flames illuminate the scene with imperfect animation while, in the tub, objects catch fire, sizzle and melt into one another, coalescing into shapeless masses of cardboard, cloth and plastic. The group joins hands and begins to sing again in thin voices which reverberate across the empty parking lot. They are singing "A Mighty Fortress Is Our God."

A Little Talent, A Lot of Desire

While records burn in that church parking lot, a few hundred miles north another group is catching fire. This group, an eight-member rock band patterned after the popular group Chicago, is performing before an enthusiastic crowd. Saddled with the unlikely name Mother Rush, they are well on their way to becoming an established musical entity in the Midwest. Big concert dates, recording contracts and thousands of screaming fans loom large in the ambitions of the eight musicians.

I know. I shared those dreams of glitter and glory. I was one of Mother's eight unruly children, and lead guitar player for the group.

I had played the guitar since I put down my bass clarinet in the school band (no future in that) and picked up a secondhand arch-top guitar that belonged to my younger brother. Before long I just *had* to have one for myself. I saved money like a miser and went electric a few months later. I began joining neighborhood groups in a kind of musical evolutionary process. Natural selection, survival of the fittest, guaranteed that the more dedicated or talented members of these neighborhood groups would stay with the music. The merely curious were weeded out after a while, leaving the serious gloryhounds to make the music. The cream rose to the top, so to speak.

I came through the evolution. What little native talent I had was considerably augmented by my intense desire to succeed in music. My dedication carried me through five combo incarnations—five different groups with different members. The only thing any of them had in common was the music, the long hours huddled in someone's garage or basement listening to records over and over again trying to capture the sound. Imitation may be the sincerest form of flattery; it is also a short-cut musical education.

By the time I reached college I considered giving up music, thinking instead in terms of a steady job to pay the college bills. I decided to sell my equipment to a new group which was just starting.

I was told to talk to Mike, the leader and organizer of this new venture. The next night I showed up at the dorm to meet Mike and make a quick sale; I was anxious to secure my college future for at least another year. Instead, I was offered an audition. It seemed that Mike was not happy with the usual crowd of pickers who had been tramping through his dorm room, guitar cases in hand. I went out and borrowed a friend's acoustic and came back a few minutes later to play some of the flashiest bits and pieces I had picked up over the years. To my great surprise and immediate dismay, I was hired.

"You're in, if you want in," Mike said.

"What about my equipment?" I asked. I still had visions of dollar signs dancing in my head.

"Well," Mike smiled, "if you join the group, you'll be needing your equipment, won't you?" True enough. I was hooked.

I went home that night with a list of songs I was to learn before showing up for the as-yet-unnamed group's first practice.

On the Road with Mother

Mother Rush—the name meant nothing to us, whatever odd images it may conjure up—was founded on one basic principle: professionalism. Everything about the group was to be professional. In fact, I was the only member not majoring in music. We even had an accountant who sent us weekly checks and paid our expenses. We also tried a novel idea—actually learning some songs before attempting to line up an audience. Most groups I had been in had been so hungry for attention, and jobs so hard to come by, that finding a "gig" usually preceeded any serious musical effort. (There is a sort of backward logic in that: if you don't ever get a job, you don't need to learn any music.)

We learned two hours worth of material—the latest Top 40 songs—and then hit the road. The first few times we played were showcase (a euphemism for *free*) concerts around the college. Within six months we were the hottest group in the immediate vicinity. In a year's time we were one of the top choices for the college and university circuit in the state, and were building a substantial following from forays into surrounding states as well. Soon there were agents and publicity and talk of record deals.

14

In the end we elected to quit while we were still ahead, splitting the money we had been saving to pay for demo tapes, more sound equipment and a bus.

So Mother Rush faded from the scene. I had been further into rock than some of my music friends, and certainly further than the general population. Like the people I played for, I had grown up on rock music. But I had also grown up in the church. I had become a Christian in high school—somehow never considering anything wrong with being a Christian and a rock musician at the same time.

After the band broke up, I did not think about playing rock 'n' roll seriously anymore. As much as I enjoyed it, that part of my life had reached a natural conclusion and was put aside. I did not become a musician; I became a writer (another interest I had been pursuing for an equally long time). After attending Northern Baptist Theological Seminary, I joined the staff of *Campus Life* magazine.

As an editor for *Campus Life* I created the "First Impressions" music review column. As I typed that first column I hardly guessed that I would soon be thrust into the front lines of an active, ongoing skirmish.

Clearly, there was a smoldering, sputtering smokepot of a war which erupted from time to time in the flames and heat of combat. From the moment that first column hit the streets the contest began. Letters poured in: angry, indignant, worried, supportive, challenging.

Letters, I Get Letters
I received hundreds of letters as a record reviewer. They may not have been overly gentle, but most were sincere. Here is a sampling:

Your approval of rock music is both deceiving and very dangerous. You have evidently not evaluated the devas-

15

tating impact of its disturbing backbeats, sensual rhythms and corrupt lyrics from any Christian point of view.
K. C.

I am very dismayed at your attempt to pollute the Christian's life by introducing worldly and un-Christlike music in your magazine. I believe many sincere Christians will be misled by your attempt to mix the lusts of secular music with the love of our Lord Jesus Christ.
C. D.

Your endorsement of rock music—hard, soft or otherwise —is not up to the quality and Christian standards your magazine has upheld in the past. Scientists tell us that rock music is harmful, so how can you decide to disagree with our Lord and science and choose to lead teens the way you want, regardless?
R. W.

I like your new column "First Impressions," but I was shocked to see rock albums included in it!
D. D.

If "First Impressions" is going to be a regular part of Campus Life, *then cancel our church's subscription. Why can't you take a stand against artists who record songs that advocate sex, the use of drugs or put down our country? The Christian sector continues to go under the pressure of the world and it looks as though you will be going with them.*
K. D.

Of course, not every letter was critical. Many endorsed the column enthusiastically, saying things like:

16

As I read "First Impressions," I was greatly encouraged in discovering that a major Christian publication was printing objective, discerning and knowledgeable record reviews.
D. L.

Thank you for "First Impressions." There is almost no other magazine I've seen or read that gives an honest view of records–rock or religious. Stick in there.
S. W.

I'm tired of reading negative responses to your new column, "First Impressions." I think you need some encouragement. Let's face it, the majority of us teen-agers, Christian or not, listen to rock. Any help in picking good rock is very much appreciated by me.
I. D.

Positive or negative, the letters kept coming in from readers all over the country—ministers, parents, youth workers, young people—drawing fresh steam from each month's column. Here were glimpses of a conflict that was much more widespread than I had realized. Even the supporters of my column were disturbed by some of the questions raised by the more vocal antirock constituency.

I began to ask myself some of my critics' questions. Was there a place for rock music? Was it, as some said, dangerous? Is there something morally wrong with listening to rock? Could it really affect us in ways we do not understand? Is there such a thing as Christian rock?

I took these questions to people I thought would be able to give me some answers, Christians in the recording industry. Some of those I talked with shared my questions and concerns, others offered helpful perspective. But the general attitude was expressed by one record company president who told me, "I don't want to talk about that; that's old stuff. I'm through with that." In essence he was saying that enough has been said already; rock is a dead issue with Christians.

But the letters told me it was not as dead as I and some others thought. Contemporary music, especially rock, continues to stir up deep feelings. Just because some in the record industry have stopped talking about it does not mean the questions have gone away.

Questions in Search of Answers

You turn on "Midnight Special" and see a group dressed in unisex jumpsuits, their faces caked in make-up and hair frizzed into electrified fright wigs. They play a grating metallic music enunciated by harsh screams and a droning beat that suggests the music was written by a robot on a bad day. All the while their leader prances around, leering at the audience, contorting his face grotesquely. They end their selection by going limp—mechanical men whose mechanism has run down—while their leader stumbles to the floor to lay twitching like an electrocution victim, groaning out the song's last few words.

Or you overhear a group talking about the latest Kiss concert, complete with firebombs, smoke and explosions. They laugh, recounting bass player Gene Simmons vomiting blood all over himself and setting the stage curtains afire with his flame thrower. The drummer levitates on his hydraulic drum riser, and the others strut and pose, threatening to topple off their six-inch stacked-heel shoes at any second. All that plus songs about masochism, sadism, prostitution, orgies, drunkenness and lust make you think a concert with Kiss is close to a night in hell.

Maybe you catch yourself humming a catchy little tune, and suddenly realize it deals not too subtly with the gay

Paul McCartney

life as presented by a group of obstensibly clean-cut characters with a penchant for dressing up as cowboys, Indians, construction workers, motorcycle cops and the like. What is going on here?

You look around and the groups keep getting weirder and crazier. The radio cranks out songs more blatant and suggestive than ever, laying bare the sex act, proclaiming the virtues of one-night stands, wondering at the perverse and unnatural. Musicians seem to care little about their audiences and openly brag about the money they will make by ripping off their fans. They live hyped-up lives filled with pills and booze and parties.

Some of the groups and artists (Barry Manilow, Paul McCartney and Wings, Linda Ronstadt, Kansas) do not seem so bad, but how can you tell? You like popular music, but what is it doing to you? Where is it leading you? Do you have to give up listening to that Foreigner, Boston or Eagles album because some people say you should?

In the rest of part one I hope to make some sense out of the confusing rock scene. In chapters two and three I discuss the image and illusion of rock and how these affect listeners. The fourth and fifth chapters cover the rhythm in rock, its origin and effects. Chapter six concerns the message of rock.

Part two examines rock in a Christian context. Chapter seven considers the issues of worldliness in relation to Christian rock music. The next chapter looks at whether rock is inherently less spiritual than other forms of music while chapter nine considers if the gospel is compromised by tying it to rock. The last chapter gives a number of criteria for judging the quality of music and the truth of its message.

The appendix gives a brief history of rock music since the 1950s. Some may find it helpful to read this first to get an overview of rock before going into the rest of the book. It can also be referred to from time to time as needed while the book is being read.

There are some hard issues in these pages. Many are not easily resolved. But they are important enough to deserve a careful and reasoned analysis under the eye of God. Let's see if we can't make some sense out of rock.

2

THE ARTFUL ILLUSION

YOU ARE SITTING IN A jam-packed concert hall. Slowly, the house lights dim and a voice booms out, "Ladies and Gentlemen, we proudly present. . . ." Suddenly the darkened stage leaps to life under a flash of white light, and there is the performer, shimmering in your gaze in a rhinestone and sequins blaze. The music starts, stirring you, lifting you. It is so enticing, so glamorous, so thoroughly exciting, you think a life of spotlights, fancy clothes and appearances before thousands of adoring fans would be just about perfect. The exhilaration, the thrill of applause washing over you in enthusiastic waves. . . .

Stars Get in Your Eyes

Problem: Rock music is fashioned and promoted in a highly attractive manner. The glitter and glamour conceal rock's true rebellious and antisocial nature.

As a musician, I traveled with Mother Rush hundreds of miles every week. We would meet Thursday or Friday afternoon to load our equipment into a U-Haul trailer. Then we would pack our bags and pile into the van and head out on the highway. The next sixty hours would be nonstop—nonstop travel, nonstop togetherness, nonstop monotony, nonstop boredom—until we rolled in again at five o'clock Sunday morning.

After a while all the motels and diners and gas stations look the same. The road wears on you. The empty hours wear on you. Typically, a musician spends twenty-two hours a day waiting for two hours of life in the spotlight. And the waiting is deadening.

But part of the illusion of show business is that the glitter of the lights touches every area of the performer's life. This illusion is as far removed from reality as tennis is from tea. The spotlight hides more than it reveals. The life of a performer is difficult, sometimes intolerable and often dull. Yet we never wanted for enthusiastic friends and followers to tag along with us on band trips. There were often so many people crammed into the van that we dubbed it the Rolling Armpit, for obvious reasons.

The fantasy of the spotlight attracts many people, especially young people. For those not acquainted with the reality of the road, it is often difficult to separate the illusion (the image of glamour and prestige) from the art (making music). This is not surprising, since most performers insist on creating and maintaining their own variation of the illusion, cutting out larger-than-life

24

Rod Stewart

figures for themselves.

Mick Jagger and the Rolling Stones adopt an air of arrogance and decadence. The Eagles become outlaws. Peter Frampton projects the image of rock's darling. Elton John claims Captain Fantastic status. These are all poses, images. Of course, this is a necessary part of show business. We all want our entertainers and stars to be the biggest and the best, at least different from us in some obvious way. We want those vicarious thrills we get seeing "somebody." An ordinary nobody does not rate a second look. It is no wonder performers put on a glittery front.

But there is a problem when we can no longer distinguish the illusion from reality, the image from the art. Sometimes this happens with the performers themselves. They begin to think of themselves as the characters they play. More often it happens with us, the audience; we think what we see on stage is the real person.

Rock musicians are good image manipulators. By and large they work hard to create an image (all-American boy, rebel, darling, pervert or weirdo) and constantly enhance and reinforce it by their actions. Most performers are happy with this arrangement. Since their public life bears little resemblance to their private life, the artfully contrived image can actually protect their privacy. In performance they can slip into their image, showing that to their fans, and leave their personal lives safe from prying eyes. The greater the distance between their real life and their stage personality, the more secure their privacy.

Rebels without a Cause

In the early days of rock 'n' roll, the musicians were cast as rebels. Rock was called the music of rebellion, though in real life the musicians were not rebelling much against anything. Trouble started when people began paying too much attention to the image.

The rebel image of early rock 'n' roll got a lot of publicity in the popular press. The music *was* different. Bill Haley and the Comets stumbled onto a hybrid blend of country western and swing that had a special appeal. Their recording of "Rock around the Clock" in 1955 became the first rock 'n' roll record to achieve number one national status. (Although the phrase "rock 'n' roll" had been introduced in 1951 by deejay Alan Freed as a term for his radio show, it had not caught hold as yet.) "Rock around the Clock" made Bill Haley rock's first superstar. Fans rallied to him, a slightly overweight, comical, benign uncle-figure, quite unused to the commotion he seemed to cause wherever he went.

The crazy acceptance of Haley and his innocuous music kicked off the rebellion image in music. The underdog's struggle against authority had become a popular literary theme and was reinforced in movies such as *Rebel without a Cause* and *Blackboard Jungle*. The latter included a scene in which Haley and his Comets played their hit, "Rock around the Clock," making it the first rock movie.

Blackboard Jungle, about a teacher who struggles to impart some basic values to a group of hardened, streetwise kids only to be rebuffed, was released to pandemonium. Fans loved it; critics and authorities hated it. Russia denounced it as a capitalistic plot to subvert their children. In Britain it caused riots in the streets. Elsewhere it was publicly condemned and the film confiscated by various local authorities. For this and other reasons, rock music was quickly branded as outlaw music—an image which has sometimes increased its popularity and at other times limited its appeal, but one which it has never managed to shake.

If Bill Haley was not particularly outlawish in his

27

baggy pants, plaid sportscoat and string tie, along came Elvis with his dark, smoldering good looks, greased-back hair and dangerously curled lip. Elvis radiated a sex appeal which made Haley look like an old shoe. Adults could not stand Elvis, making him all the more desirable as a prime teen commodity. Adult resentment grew into a fierce dislike and, consequently, Elvis's success was assured.

Newspapers and magazines reported Elvis's every sneer. They were warming to the idea of rock stars and rock 'n' roll as a great source of lively, controversial stories. By 1956 rock 'n' roll stories were common, taking one of two forms: "Let's all pooh-pooh the new lunacy," or "Rock 'n' roll is taking us to hell in a handbasket." Still, most people figured that rock 'n' roll was merely an unfortunate fad, and would soon go the way of goldfish-swallowing, jitterbugging and phone-booth stuffing.

But time rolled on and rock had no intention of giving up the backbeat as quickly as predicted. The media which had forecast its death every year since its beginning took on a new slant. Silly stories ("Look what the crazies are doing now!") ceased, and outright attacks became common. Decent citizens took arms against the "child corrupters." It did not matter if rock 'n' roll was rebellious in content or not, a rebellion formed around it. Soon it became an act of defiance just to listen to rock 'n' roll music. The antisocial image grew and so did the tension surrounding it.

This tension has continued in one form or another, hot and cold. Periodically, groups like the Osmonds, Jacksons or ABBA, or singers like Barry Manilow, John Denver or Olivia Newton-John came along to launder rock's soiled image and put on a well-scrubbed front. Yet something or someone else also came along to besmirch the newly polished image and drag it through the mud again. The folly is that all this energy is focused on the illusion.

All the World a Stage

Rock musicians are actors. The world of contemporary culture is their stage. What they say about themselves and their music is like so many lines from a continuing play. Bob Dylan used to tell people that he was an orphan and a vagabond to hide the fact that he was from Minnesota, and his family was named Zimmerman. Elton John, his career starting to taper off a bit, released a juicy tidbit of information: "I'm bisexual." Zap! Elton is the center of attention again as the press buzzes with shock and indignation. ("Hey, did you hear about Elton John?" "Yeah, I was reading in the papers about it. Weird.") Performers are creating and enhancing their illusions all the time; not everything they say should be gullibly swallowed whole.

Although the performers may know where the illusion leaves off and reality begins, often the general public does not. We are left to struggle with the illusion, which is all we see. Still, in fighting the illusion, wrestling with the image, real conflict often develops, conflict which can divide families and cause deep emotional wounds. There were sometimes more fireworks in an evening discussing some of my music with my parents than Kiss uses in a month—and my folks at least tried to understand!

Sadly, much of the conflict is unnecessary. It can be avoided once we get a handle on some of the main problem areas. To accurately understand rock, we must penetrate the illusion, separate the image (rebellion, violence, glamour or whatever) from the reality (making music).

Consider, for example, professional wrestling which relies heavily on show-biz tactics to draw spectators. Wrestlers with names like Mad Dog, the Masked Assassin or the Screaming Russian strut before the camera, foaming at the mouth with false bravado and wild promises of may-

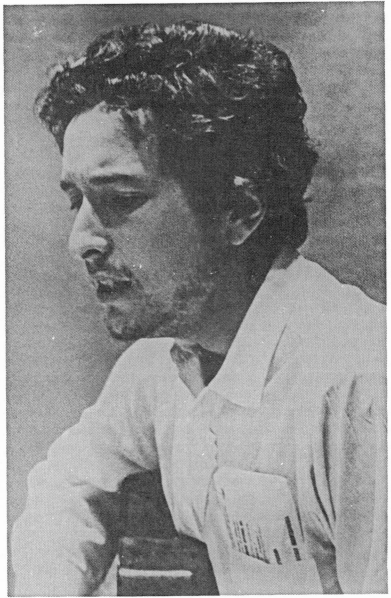

Bob Dylan

hem, disgrace, humiliation and defeat for their enemies. "I'll break that guy's neck, so help me. If I ever get my hands on him, I'll kill him! After what happened in Kansas City, he's running scared and he knows it. This will be the match of the century...."

If anyone dreamed that these maniacs were serious, none of them would be allowed to walk the streets. But professional wrestling is so transparently phony, the theatrics are so old and clichéd, no one believes them. If you wanted to talk about the *sport* of professional wrestling, you would quickly discard the two-bit dramatics. In a sense, that is what I would like to do with music— deflate the illusions and talk about the "sport," the music known as rock.

Actually, pro wrestling and rock have more in common than we might first realize. Both are firmly rooted in the entertainment business. Look at the rockers of the sixties, or at today's new wave and punk rock scene and you will find the same elements found in pro wrestling—insane bragging and arrogance, absurd posturing, contrived exploitation of the media for publicity, cultivation of outlandish appearances and bizarre behavior. Even their names have the same cornball ring of the melodramatic: The Dead Boys, Sex Pistols, Devo, Voidoids, Dictators, B-52s. The only major difference is that professional wrestlers are known for the phonies they are, while unfortunately rock musicians are taken more seriously. They should not be.

Think of rock music and all its trappings as a big navel orange. If you want to eat the orange, you must peel away the thick, indigestible rind to get to the fruit. If you tried to eat the orange *without* peeling it, you would get a very wrong impression of the fruit. The taste and texture would be too confusing to enjoy. It is much the same with rock. For any discussion to have meaning, we must, as much as possible, peel away the images and illusions which confuse the issue, and separate them from the notes-on-paper music. The meat of the fruit is what we want to talk about, not the peeling. Unfortunately, when some people set out to talk rock, they take one bite of the rind and declare how bad the fruit tastes.

Admittedly, this is a difficult task, but the best way to peel away the illusions is to develop a healthy, open-minded skepticism. Be skeptical of all you see and hear in rock music.

Suppose a quartet of guitar hackers in silver spangled jumpsuits declared, "Now is the time for violent revolution! We are going to take over the world with our guitars!" A proper response might be, "Oh, really?"

Coming from a Hitler, that statement might have some meaning. Coming from a group of immature, ego-tripping rock musicians, it is nonsense. Yet, groups have come up with ludicrous statements like that (and worse), and people, not realizing they were dealing with one of rock's more potent illusions, have reacted as if Hitler himself were speaking.

Books, articles and pamphlets have been written about the subversive, communistic tactics of rock. That probably makes the rockers who dreamed up those comments ecstatic. They wanted attention, and look what they got! We have to be careful not to attribute to such statements validity they do not deserve. Luckily, most people are skeptical enough to doubt that a tin-eared tribe of pop musicians could take over the world with their guitars and drums. The truth is, even the most radical groups are content merely to renegotiate their recording contracts successfully.

This is not to say that some performers do not attempt to

use their real or imagined power to influence their fans. For example, a number of rock musicians and performers have come out strongly against nuclear power proliferation. "No Nukes!" they say at concerts which raise money for the cause. In the sixties, many groups attempted to sway the balance of political power in this country. Joan Baez and Peter, Paul and Mary and many others got involved in the anti-Vietnam War effort.

Whenever entertainers attempt to use their public image to sway popular opinion we should be wary. We need to ask ourselves, "What does this musician know about _____?" Fill in the blank: nuclear power, saving whales, electing a president, banning the bomb, stopping a war, legalizing marijuana. All these issues and more have been espoused by rock performers from time to time.

Of course, everyone is allowed free voice to his or her ideas. But we must carefully scrutinize any public personality (rock musician, sports hero, television star, movie actor) who ascends to the soapbox. A skeptical outlook is a basic requirement for all of us living in the media age.

Since rock musicians are image manipulators, most often what they say and do is calculated for a purpose. Usually that purpose is attention. They want to stand out from the crowd, to be noticed. Some artists, it seems, will say or do anything to be noticed, the more bizarre and shocking the better. So they dye their hair green, dress like space cadets, talk about overthrowing the empire, or advocate free atomic waste for first graders—whatever will give the most attention at the time. A skeptical person knows these antics to be nothing more than strands of the illusion which are important to the artist because they help obscure the all-too-plain truth that, ultimately, rock

33

stars are just ordinary people. Beneath the eye shadow and glitter, they are much like the rest of us.

Alice Cooper is fairly well known for his shocking stage performances—such as beheadings, cavorting with live snakes, hangings, surrealistic nightmare sequences. But Vincent Furier (Alice's real name) does not sit around at home wearing torn leotards and grotesque facial make-up. According to numerous interviews, he plays golf, softball, watches television and goes about his life much the same as anyone else. His life off stage is dull compared to what he projects in the spotlight.

If we are skeptical, we should also keep an open mind about rock. True, rock artists may be image manipulators, but they are also style shapers with an eye to the future. Who could have guessed that the Beatles, with their natty suits and shaggy locks, would spark a major revolution in the way men dress today? And who could have foreseen the tremendous repercussions this style revolution has caused? However, in the beginning nearly everyone was shocked by their appearance. For some, the shock wore off quickly, replaced with eager acceptance and enthusiastic imitation. And now, years later, even the harshest critics of the Beatles' early appearance are sporting the effects: longer hairstyles, more colorful and better tailored clothing. It all seems harmless now.

We must learn to keep an open mind, to balance our skepticism, about rock and its illusions. Times change and bring new concerns to the fore, which seem as important as longer hair once did. We must ask if they really are important. To discuss rock music seriously we must be aware of the illusions and not get caught up in the superficial trappings such as hair, clothes, language and styles of life. Keeping an open mind and a skeptical outlook will help us to debunk much of the nonsense and concentrate our

34

attention on the real issues which, unlike professional wrestling, do exist in rock.

Promoting the Pop Product

Part of the reason it is so difficult to separate the illusion from reality is because rock music, like any other product of pop culture, promotes its illusions as the product itself. In other words, they aren't selling the steak, they're selling the sizzle.

Rock music is a product—records bought and sold in shiny, alluring jackets featuring beautiful people. They are advertised, promoted, pumped up, hyped for all they are worth (and far beyond their worth). There is music mixed in too, but the larger commodity being sold is the experience, the atmosphere, the status of owning the product. And since rock music is the expression of a quickly changing culture, immediacy is a large part of the package. This week's No. 1 hit! Hottest group in the U.S. Buy it now! (Next month it will be off the charts and the group, has-beens.)

Rock as a commodity is packaged in an attractive way that has little to do with the music. It is strictly commercial. These same people would sell hotcakes if there was as much money in it.

The issue is not that the attractive package conceals rock's dangerous side but rather that the package has become the product. It is not that unsuspecting people are being sold something they do not want or would not buy if they were told the truth. No, people buy rock because they *want* what the package offers. In a vicarious way they want to participate in the illusion of glamour, excitement and fast living which the promotion promises, which the music appears to deliver.

In a very unsettling way the illusion has become the

35

reality. Rock music, since it is a creature of the moment, spawned in fury and nurtured by heroes of enchanted lives, lends itself easily to whatever illusion surrounds it. It is a chameleon which becomes part of the scenery, taking on the color of the moment.

At this level it becomes nearly impossible to separate the illusion from the art. They are the same thing. Here, too, is where the utmost in open-minded skepticism is called for. Fortunately, most people are naturally skeptical and levelheaded enough not to want to emulate all the weirdness going on in the rock 'n' roll world. But some do.

Some, through an unfulfilled need for attention, belonging, esteem or whatever, do seek to copy in their sphere of reality what they see taking place in the rock world. This is the problem.

But it is a problem much larger than rock music itself. It is a social problem that extends to modern culture at large and finds expression not only in music but in such unlikely things as automobiles, alcohol, sports and fashion, in anything which touches culture and can be packaged and sold as a product.

Rock is seen as more of a threat, however, because it offers shelter for certain antisocial tendencies. Therefore, it draws more concern than, say, the fact that certain grown men buy little snazzy sports cars to go zooming around town like Mario Andretti—they don't hurt anybody. But the guy who wants to do drugs because his favorite rock star does drugs can get hurt.

The person who comes stoned to a rock concert is suffering from the same malady as the person who goes crazy over designer jeans. But again that has little to do with rock music itself, or clothes either. Banning rock 'n' roll is not the solution any more than preventing the sale

36

of Calvin Kleins or Gloria Vanderbilts.

The beginning of a solution is to use the faculties already mentioned that are available to us: open-mindedness and skepticism. They can give us enough perspective to see that we can indeed "live" without a pair of Calvin Kleins or the latest Rolling Stone album. Where those faculties are lacking in someone we know, someone who seems in danger of going overboard, we can speak up, helping one another to disentangle the illusions from the realities. Of course, that is much more difficult than simply declaring, "No more rock music!" It takes sensitivity, tact and compassion. The same ingredients are needed to solve any human problem.

3

STARMAKER MACHINERY

IDOL WORSHIP IN AMERICA has always taken a novel approach. Our idols of stage and screen are lifted to fantastic heights on waves of popular appeal, only to be tossed over at the first sign of a new hero. The average life of a star is about two years; superstars last a little longer.

But while riding the crest of popularity, a superstar's influence seems awesome. Whether the image is illusion or not, the power seems quite real.

Rock musicians often enjoy the same social status as movie stars or politicians. They all walk in worlds of larger-than-life dimensions where every move is publicized and reported by the gossip columnists. "Fanzines" (fan magazines) spew out a never-ending stream of thick, syrupy sensationalism over the moment's heart-throb.

The lives of these superluminaries are magnified by the constant scrutiny of an everwatchful press and public. It has been said, "The camera never blinks." Neither does the public eye.

Occasionally, the public becomes indignant over what it sees transpiring in these golden lives. Rock stars are notorious for stirring up the public ire in one way or another.

Hear No Evil, See No Evil, Speak No Evil

Problem: The lives of rock musicians are morally corrupt. Since these stars are worshiped by their fans, their immoral actions have a great impact. Basic human values are undermined and their followers are influenced steadily toward immorality.

A thousand years ago small groups of uncultivated, bizarrely dressed, oddly named musicians traveled from town to town, singing and accompanying themselves on the vielle [a stringed instrument]. The most famous of these—Jumping Hare, Little String, Ladies Praiser and Rainbow—were rewarded with such fame and luxury that they were imitated by hordes of less gifted, envious men. During the late Middle Ages chronicles refer to "large armies of minstrels," the better ones playing for nobility while lesser troupes entertained at peasant celebrations. Despite the demand for their performances at all levels of society, these itinerant poet-musicians were held in contempt throughout the era. The animosity stemmed principally from the Church, which held that their obvious secular joie de vivre [joy of living] posed a threat to the spiritual welfare of its people.[1]

It would seem that we have not changed much in a thousand or so years. Migrating armies of musicians still roam

40

the land. The more famous make huge heaps of money and live in luxury, to be imitated by the less gifted who also strive to make great piles of money and live in luxury. And the whole scheme is held in contempt by the collective moral conscience.

Popular music has often been seen as an eroding agent on humanity's spiritual well-being, a rat in the cellar gnawing at the "new-wine" keg. Popular musicians have often been cast in the role of Pied Piper, leading their all-too-willing followers down the primrose path to sin.

The question of influence is really a knotty problem, bound up as it is with theories of human development, cultural considerations, morality, values and various items of media luggage. The question at the root, "How is human behavior influenced?" opens onto such an untidy landscape of current thought that the temptation is to steer by the most obvious landmarks and pass through as quickly as possible.

While some rock stars merely cultivate an immoral image, others are actually immoral. Do immoral rock artists have a bad influence on their fans? "Yes, of course," we say, and move on to something else, such as how much money and fame their displayed immorality brings them. But the issue is much more complex than that, demanding a more thorough examination.

Mold Me. Make Me. Just Don't Break Me!

The prevailing view of human development posits that one's parents are the single most influential force in a person's life. Further, it is suggested that within a relatively short time, a few months to a few years, the individual is endowed with the major portion of his or her personality components and most, if not all, of his or her moral values. Most psychological theorists suggest that we become what

41

we are, and what we will be, at a very early age. Some say as early as the age of five, others indicate later on, somewhere between eleven and fourteen. Whatever the case, the formative years are extremely important; we change only slowly and with difficulty after then.

But people *do* change, for better or worse despite what kind of upbringing they may have had.

Research into personality development shows that people are most vulnerable to influence and, therefore, to change in the areas of their greatest needs. On a physical level we all need food to survive. If we were long without food, we would become vulnerable to the influence of anyone who promised to give us food. In the same way we are vulnerable on a psychological level. We all have basic psychological needs: acceptance, self-esteem, affection. If these basic needs are denied or withheld, we become vulnerable to the influence of anyone or anything which promises to provide us with those feelings.

As we get older we look to fulfill our needs more and more apart from our families. Thus, personal friends and peers become ever more important, and we become more vulnerable to their influence. We look for role models to imitate, trying various possibilities before settling into the one which wears the most comfortably.

People are not chameleons, however, forever changing to fit the demands of their surroundings. Eventually, mature human beings emerge which stand on their own apart from parents or peers. The time for role models passes as the soft core of mutability hardens into a solid personal identity. Still, from time to time, the solidified personality is vulnerable to change depending upon various outer and inner circumstances. More and more we realize that people are open to change throughout their lives at certain intervals for brief periods of time.

42

These intervals could be thought of as windows which open and close periodically throughout life. When the windows are open the personality is extremely vulnerable to influence. When the windows are closed, the personality actually resists change and is somewhat invulnerable to whatever influences may gather outside.

The windows of vulnerability are open wide during the first months and years of life, they close slowly and remain closed until the beginning of adolescence when they again open wide. The windows close again after adolescence and open a crack only briefly at the beginning of young adulthood. The windows of vulnerability will open several times more before old age. Of course, the windows of vulnerability can be forcibly opened by any number of very strong circumstances brought to bear on the personality.

The most important interval is the one during adolescence when tremendous mental, physical and emotional upheavals begin, and when the larger world outside the family takes on great attraction—when rock music becomes a magic carpet to an individual fantasy world populated with scores of like-minded, like-bodied, like-spirited comrades.

Pop Goes the Culture

There is a large, active and aggressive youth culture in this country. Perhaps in no other time in history has there been so much available to so many at such a young age. Those entering the youth culture are delighted to discover their own clothing styles, language, entertainment and rules of behavior provided for them. And young people all participate to varying degrees in this highly sophisticated, highly complex youth culture.

At the same time, this is a totally pluralistic culture,

capable of sheltering and supporting many different roles, modes of behavior, world views and lifestyles. People with absolutely nothing in common in regard to upbringing, education or economic status can find common ground in the youth culture merely because they are young and share the desire to experiment with life. This is the strength of the youth culture and the very thing which terrifies parents and moral leaders. The window is wide open for absolutely anything to come in.

While young people may make up the youth culture and participate in it, they do not actually create it. Instead, the various elements of the youth culture are copied or recycled from the larger adult community, or are devised especially for young people by adults, as in the case of clothing, entertainment, cosmetics and other accouterments. Although the youth culture may willingly embrace these trappings, they tend to be dictated to them by older tastemakers. This happens in ads directly (entertainment and clothes) and indirectly (cars, liquor and cigarettes).

Thus, a young person can show up at a favorite rock-concert arena wearing the clothes from a favorite magazine, talking like a favorite television character, drinking the beer of a favorite football player, acting out erotic scenarios from favorite movies.

Many adults and moral leaders, alarmed by what they see taking place among the young, look for an explanation for all the negative things they see going on: drinking, promiscuity, drugs, rebellion: "After all," they say, "We didn't teach them to act this way. It must be those rock performers!"

That is a simple, plausible explanation. But the problem is more complex. Young people are not exactly powerless pawns of culture; they influence it and it influences them. By their acceptance or rejection of various elements, they continually transform the culture that surrounds them. What may appear from the outside to be a vast, impenetrable private domain is really a highly transient, unstable sea of change when seen from within. The tributaries which feed this sea are innumerable, or nearly so. Everything of modern life finds its way into the cultural mix.

The emerging diagram of influence can be seen as a spiral. As young people enter the youth culture they come under its influence and in turn exert influence upon it, changing it only to be further influenced, and so on. Does the spiral ever stop? No, but people eventually stop responding to the influence of culture; they simply grow out of it. Their windows of vulnerability close, and they are left with whatever they brought in.

This is the scary part: what if the things which are brought in are personally damaging, morally reprehensible or socially unacceptable?

Some say that music, like other forms of art, does not influence culture, but simply reflects it. Others say that a powerful, dynamic art form such as rock music goes far beyond merely reflecting its culture to actively influencing it. The truth is, I think, somewhere between those two poles.

Performers know what their audiences want to hear and try to deliver the goods (reflection); they also know that to remain popular they have to stay just a half-step ahead (influence). It is a cat-and-mouse game played on intuition.

Many performers, however, exploit the current trend to cash in on the sound of the moment. That is commercialization. In some ways commercialization fosters an acceptance of its subject by misrepresenting its true size or na-

45

ture. For example, the maker of the country's fifth-ranked soda pop frequently airs a television commercial that shows *everyone* in an entire village drinking that brand, simultaneously! "Jump on the bandwagon! Be part of the gang; don't get left behind!" That is the commercial appeal. Commercialism can work in music just as it works with soda pop, by distorting the music's importance. Since popular music is basically commercial music, it would seem that its power to influence, to move people to act, is enormous.

More and more, the forces of culture display a distinct and relentless pull toward the negative. The vulnerable individual is overwhelmed by a gravitational field too strong to resist and too enticing to avoid. More and more, the end is a vulnerable personality which has crash-landed on a harsh and alien world whose fragile craft is now damaged beyond repair. Stranded. Lost. Prey to a host of modern horrors.

Here is a problem far larger in scope than many realize. It is not enough to be concerned merely with removing the more obviously obnoxious elements of a culture, striking out at the sensational and salacious. That is like the first mate passing out galoshes on the tilting deck of the Titanic; it shows little appreciation of the true nature and magnitude of the problem. The issue is reduced to ridiculous simplicity, rendering any treatment of it inexact, ineffective and inconsequential.

The problem of creeping immorality in our society simply cannot be cured by removing a relative handful of rock 'n' roll renegades. Anyone who suggests that it can is like a one-pill doctor bent on treating a score of maladies with a single stock remedy. Not only is the result ordained to failure, it can actually endanger the patient.

A Legend in Our Own Time

As I have said, the youth culture is highly transient. Although it appears very solid and impenetrable from the outside, it is a very fluid, changing culture. This reflects in part the physical quality of young people—they grow up, leaving the youth culture behind. It also in part explains the short attention span granted to most rock stars. Once at the top of his or her career, the rock star is only too quickly replaced by another, newer face, as a younger contingent enters the scene and seeks a hero that conforms more closely to its tastes.

What of the old rock star? If he does not fade from the scene completely, he may retain a considerable number of his loyal following. As the star grows older, so do his fans, many of whom will continue being fans till his dying day. This does not mean that the older, adult culture will necessarily approve of the star or his music anymore. It just means that as the adult culture gives way to the new generation, dissenting voices will be somewhat muted and eventually silenced.

To see how this works, let us examine one of the legends of our own time: Elvis.

Elvis, at his height, was everywhere at once, and his fans were legion, screaming hordes of teen-agers, crying, dying for a look at him. His concerts are now famous. Tony Palmer recounts, "He came on leering and twitching, his hair all down in his eyes, his grin lopsided. The moment the music started he went berserk. Spasms rocked his body as if it had been plugged into the same electrical source as his guitar. His hips began to grind, his legs vibrated like power drills. He pouted and humped and walked as if he were sneering with his legs."[2]

Television producers allowed him only to be shown from the waist up. Neither Ed Sullivan nor Steve Allen would

47

Elvis Presley

risk the public outrage by showing Elvis undiluted; he was just too strong for family viewing.

From the beginning it seemed that nobody except his fans had any use for Elvis.

Critics loathed him, preachers called him sinful; in Miami, he was charged with obscenity; in San Diego, the city fathers voted to ban him altogether –unless he omitted from his act all "vulgar movement." A Baptist pastor in Des Moines declared him "morally insane."
According to the East German Communist paper Young World, *Elvis Presley was a "weapon of the American psychological war aimed at infecting a part of the population with a new philosophical outlook of inhumanity ... to destroy anything that is beautiful, in order to prepare for war."*[3]

How embarrassing! The communists, who had long been accused of trying to pervert our country's youth as part of their master plot to conquer the world were now leveling the same accusation at us: "Elvis is corrupting our children!" If he was, the children of the world could not have cared less.

Soon there was Elvis everything: T-shirts to toilet paper, bobby socks (flourescent, yet) and bubble gum, ball-point pens, lipstick, hound dogs and Bermuda shorts. And movies. Elvis starred in a string of smash hits which kept him before his loyal public. And the coins kept rolling in. He made $24,000 for single appearances and grossed $100,000,000 in two years.

Years passed and after several artfully contrived comebacks, Elvis remained King of the Rock, reaching the ultimate in acceptability—performing for the president of the United States. Not only did he appear before President Nixon, but (due in large part to the savvy of his manager, Colonel Tom Parker) he is probably the only

49

entertainer to receive his customary fee for a command performance. A few more years passed; then, unexpectedly, Elvis died at age forty-two. Millions mourned his passing. The King was dead. The world wept.

What happened? How did this greasy-haired kid, chief corruptor and herald to open rebellion become acceptable, even somewhat respectable?

What happened is that we just got used to Elvis. The young people of the fifties grew up with him, and the older folks, after living with him a while, decided that he was not so bad after all. Very rich and very famous (both bringing him a substantial amount of respectability), Elvis became a sort of folk hero.

Elvis did not change—our perception of him changed. He was no longer that obscene young man who was leading the world to ruin. He was the Sun King who owned a Southern mansion where tour buses full of little old ladies stopped. If you were lucky, you could scramble out and snatch a handful of gravel from his driveway, or better yet, catch a glimpse of the King himself strolling the grounds or riding his motorcycle around Graceland.

Elvis became so well accepted that on a trip to Washington, D.C., in 1970, he dropped by the headquarters of the FBI to volunteer his services as an undercover agent. It seems that Elvis was peeved at the Beatles for their "filthy, unkempt appearance and suggestive music." Elvis explained to Research Chief M. A. Jones, who interviewed him, that his own long hair and unusual appearance were merely "tools of the trade which allowed him access to and rapport with many people." Imagine that. Here is society's one-time archvillain offering to join the good guys to help stamp out the new wave of child corrupters. Director of the FBI J. Edgar Hoover later wrote Elvis a letter telling him he would "keep in mind your offer to be of assistance."[4]

50

Success, the kind Elvis had, goes a long way toward making a person respectable. Now, years after his death, Elvis is a sort of saint, and Graceland Mansion in Memphis is a shrine to pilgrims from all over the world. His life story is told and retold in a stream of movies, books and television shows.

On the Skids

Some would take the rather pessimistic view that the crazy acceptance of Elvis is ample indication of the moral decline this world is skidding into. Others might argue that we have merely grown up a bit and learned that Elvis was not so bad after all. Probably a point somewhere between the two views is close to the truth. Elvis certainly was not as evil as he was made out to be in the early days, but he did open the door for some genuinely dangerous influences to come in after him. Others would pick up the cues he laid down and push far beyond his furthest limit.

This poses a rather frightening progression: the younger members of society come into contact with increasingly rough, evermore malignant influences which face them when they are least able to withstand such forces. Capitulation, in some form, would seem almost inevitable.

Of course, it should be remembered that rock, though potent, is still only one part of the cultural mix and that all people are not affected equally by their environment. In fact, the sheer multiplicity of possible influences almost guarantees that whatever influences do reach a person will be somewhat diluted. Also, people do not interpret elements of culture in black and white terms. Always, overt stimuli are filtered through the highly individualized perceptions of the person involved, to be acted upon in any of a billion ways. Rarely are influences internalized directly and instantaneously.

Dennis Benson, a well-known rock interviewer with a syndicated radio show on over five hundred rock stations, describes a poignant example of this filtering effect.

When David Cassidy (Shaun's older brother) was popu-lar I went to his concert and I interviewed him. I also asked a young girl, about twelve or thirteen, why she "loved" David Cassidy. She said she loved the Partridge Family [*the TV show David starred in*], *which to me was the most innocuous television show I've ever seen. They worried about a hairpin being lost. I said, "Why?" and she said, "Because my dad drinks, and everyone in my family is really cruel."*

For her, the Partridge family became a model of a family who really cared about each other. Here I was making an artistic judgement about a dull, noncreative situation comedy, and she was seeing it as a family that cares so much that even little things matter. So again, you have to meet people, see where they are, what they hear, and what the music means to them.[5]

It is tragic that that young girl had nothing better to turn to than a simplistic television show for guidance. But since many parents, teachers and even church leaders have often failed to present wholesome moral values, a large number of young people are left to look to whatever source they can find. They look to their friends first and then to whoever meets them on their own ground. For some, since music speaks more forcefully to a special inner need, rock stars and rock music become significant in shaping their attitudes—hardly a comforting thought.

In the end, who can determine what the total effect of any given influence is for an individual? Is morality at the mercy of style mongers, a function of the various distilled elements of culture? Or is there some latent moral ethic engraved upon society in general which keeps it from dissolving completely into savagery with each generation? Who can say?

While behavior to a predetermined set of values can always be bought, it is often at the cost of true maturity. Therefore, ridding the world of rock music and rock musicians—even if it could be easily accomplished—is not the answer. Even to say, "No more rock music in this house," is rarely by itself a satisfactory response. For who knows what demons will rush in to fill the void?

4

ROOTS REVISITED

Rock 'n' roll streaked in on Haley's Comets in 1955 to the tune of "Rock around the Clock." Before that there had been rhythm and blues, boogie, bop, swing, New Orleans jazz, blues and ragtime, stretching back in an unbroken chain to the dark jungles of Africa where the "beat" was originally conceived centuries before.

There, in savage displays of frenzied ritual, tribes of naked, sweating men pounded out their jungle rhythms under the mesmerizing stare of demon idols. Inspired in evil and nurtured in sin, the beat flourished on the dark continent until it was transplanted to these native shores with the slaves—at least, that's the popular notion of rock's history.

This African Connection is something amateur rock

historians put a lot of faith in. It is a handy myth, and there is perhaps some truth in it. But how much?

Black Africa and the Big Beat

Problem: Rock has a strong, compelling beat. It is very dangerous since it owes its beginnings to African demon worship and may itself be demon inspired.

This problem points to the apparent similarities between rock and some of Africa's tribal music. There is no question that music is, and always has been, an important part of the lives of the African peoples. But the connection between the music of various African tribes, America's slaves and the rock music of today is not easily made.

As Alex Haley's epic, *Roots,* amply demonstrated to millions of readers and television viewers across the world, slavery in America was not a game. Men, women and children were ripped from their homes and families and stuffed into ships as cargo bound for the "land of liberty." Upon their arrival, the slaves were sold on the auction block in various ports in America.

These native African slaves brought with them certain aspects of their culture: folkways, religion, language, traditions and music. But after working in the New World for a few decades, Blacks saw they were never going to get back home and became more Western in their thinking and living.

Some would suggest that although they spoke English and considered themselves American, the slaves' music remained outside the Americanization process. Black music, they say, developed into a number of distinct styles (spirituals, blues, ragtime, jazz) and somehow managed to retain the old African influence, especially in rhythm and beat. That is where the trouble is, some say—in the beat.

56

The "Black beat," we are told, is an evil beat because it was developed in music used in heathen worship.

The basic premise is that rock music can be linked directly to the forms of music derived by Blacks.

Bob Larson, probably the leading antirock crusader, said in his book, *The Day Music Died,* "In America, rock music has its roots in jazz—an emotional music which gives vent to feelings—and in Negro gospel singing from which the rhythm and blues come." He then goes on to link the American Black with a mythical past. "It is probably incidental (though some might cite scriptural references otherwise) that the black man has fostered the music which at one time incited heathens to frenzy and cannibalism."[1]

Rock's Roots

Africa is a very big place. It has more than three times the area of the United States and even more geographical diversity. It also contains over five thousand separate peoples with perhaps as many different cultures, languages and traditions.

Various countries captured slaves from outlets all along the coasts of Africa. Most of the slaves who found their way to the United States came not from the tropical rain forests but from the northern regions of the great savannas, the area of Nigeria and the Ivory Coast. Interestingly, the drum (and therefore, "the beat") was not an important instrument in the northern region of Africa from where American slaves came. Tony Palmer in *All You Need Is Love: The Story of Popular Music,* observes, "The principal musical instruments of the savanna were stringed.... Particularly common was the *banya*." The *banya* is the father of today's banjo. Palmer also points out that the banya did not originate in Black Africa, but

57

came there by way of Egyptian caravans.[2]

Drums such as the slaves possessed were suppressed by white slave holders in America because plantation owners believed (perhaps rightly so) that the messages of revolt could be passed back and forth between groups of slaves. The banjo, on the other hand, had a brighter future as the slave's chief musical instrument since its usefulness as a telephone was almost nil.

As Palmer observes, "Drums were almost never heard in black American music until well into the twentieth century." That is, of course, several decades after the invention of jazz, blues and spirituals.[3]

Africa has contributed a great deal to American music. But musical influences are not easy to unravel; clear lines for tracing music back into uncharted history are not as neatly laid out as some think. Some music historians such as George Pullen Jackson discredit the African Connection completely by suggesting that Blacks learned their music from the Whites. Bruno Nettl in *Music in Primitive Culture* states that "Jackson has traced the history of the spiritual (forerunner of jazz and the blues) and has concluded that it originated in the Scotch-Irish and English hymnody of the South. . . . He traced Negro spirituals to white hymnbooks of the nineteenth century and concludes that Negroes learned the hymns from the whites."[4]

The belief that "the beat" stayed alive or even existed in the music of the slaves rests on a shaky foundation. It is difficult to support the idea that Black music survived in America (with no important changes) when everything else of African culture, such as language, customs, dress and religion, was either discouraged, lost or forgotten. One could make a more convincing case that the rock beat came from country-western music since the first rock songs were written and recorded by a country swing band originally known as "The Saddlemen." Under Bill Haley's leadership, this group, as we have seen, got rock rolling. He was not Black, played no jazz and came from New York.

Much that has been written against rock music is actually disguised racial hatred: racism. The words used to describe it display this fact—"jungle music," "black boogie," "demon beat" and so on. There was a time when Whites discouraged rock 'n' roll shows for the simple fact that they drew both Black and White audiences. Concerned parents did not want their children mixing with other children of another race who were the same age.

As for the charge that rock's rhythm is demon inspired, most people overlook the fact that in other places where New World slaves landed (Jamaica, Haiti, the islands of the West Indies) nothing close to rock ever evolved. If the beat was so powerful and so much a part of the musical make-up of these people, why didn't something like rock develop in the Caribbean as well? Or, to put it the other way around, why don't calypso or reggae, the popular musical styles of the islands, utilize the same rhythms?

That rock and its "evil beat" originated with the slaves of Africa is a racist notion which will not stand up. About all that can be said is this: the music which for many years has been associated with Blacks in America emerged out of the general soup of America's mixing cultures where individual influences are infinite. Jazz, like rhythm and blues, ragtime and the rest which are so often the property of Blacks, were formed in the give-and-take of many cultural backgrounds (German, Czech, French, Irish, English and others) over many years. Even the music of Africa did not originate spontaneously on its own. It was shaped by its contact with Europe, Asia and the Middle East.

To lay the origins of a music condemned for its savagery

and immorality at the feet of one racial group shows a narrow interpretation of history. Worse, it is an insidious form of prejudice and racism, one into which many people have unwittingly fallen.

But even if the rock beat did not come from Africa, it is still evil. Rock music is still a channel for the devil to work in, isn't it? This question, too, deserves an answer, which I will discuss in the next chapter.

5

I'VE GOT RHYTHM!

LIKE MOST LIVING THINGS on this planet, people are rhythmic beings. We are affected by the constant ebb and flow of life's forces: sunrise, sunset; the changing seasons; weekly, monthly and yearly cycles. Especially critical are the rhythms of our heartbeat and breathing which continue moment by moment throughout our life.

The Beat Goes On and On...

Problem: As rhythmic creatures, we cannot help but be affected by the powerful, overbearing rhythms of rock music. These rhythms short-circuit centuries of refinement and sophistication, exciting our baser primitive instincts. Subjection to rock's beat can cause harm mentally, physically and emotionally.

The beat in question is the notorious *syncopated* beat, also called a backbeat. Syncopation is a simple musical device, and a common one at that, used in a variety of musical styles including church music (such as Luther's original "A Mighty Fortress"). Syncopation is merely the accenting of a beat between the regular beats of the rhythm. You might call it misplacing the beat. It works like this: if the regular beat goes 1-2-3-4, syncopating it might make it go 1-*and*-2-*and*-3-*and*-4. Say it to yourself shouting the *"and,"* and you will get some idea of what is happening.

Most, but by no means all, rock music is written in regular 4/4 time. Syncopating the beat makes it more interesting to play and listen to. Classical music also uses syncopation, as heard in Stravinsky's well-known "Firebird Suite," Beethoven's early work and much of Schumann's. You can find examples of syncopation throughout all of classical music. It is a device often used to spice up long passages or provide an interesting change of pace. However, since the rhythms of classical music are not as prominent as they are in rock, a listener may not as easily notice when syncopation comes into play. Of course, not all rock is syncopated, but since rock is a music of few elements, the beat is very close to the surface and is easily apprehended. Rock simply relies on this common musical device to perhaps a greater degree than other forms of music.

All musical rhythm is based on the idea of anticipation. As the music unfolds, the listener's mind reviews the pattern of beats that make up the rhythm, and projects or anticipates the beats to follow. When the anticipated beat follows as expected, the listener is satisfied. Syncopation breaks up this process. The accented beat is different than what is anticipated. This is what makes rock feel jerky or impulsive to those not used to it.

The contention of many is that this truncated beat is harmful to the human organism because it upsets the natural balance, or rhythm, of the body or mind.

In the late sixties, when hard rock was at its height, many people, including doctors, psychologists, sociologists and educators, became concerned about the effects which loud noise and powerful rhythms might have on young people. Experiments were designed, samples were taken, studies were conducted, and the evidence sifted for hard facts.

One of the more famous tests involved three groups of plants. The plants in plot A got good healthy doses of classical music beamed at them all day long. Plant plot B was strafed relentlessly with hard rock. Plant plot C was a control group that heard only the sounds of mother nature herself.

The results? Plot A developed a strong affinity for classical music and grew in the direction of the speakers. Plot C grew straight and tall as average plants do. But plt B, subjected to hard rock, first turned away from the speakers and then sickened and died.

Whether this test was actually ever carried out, or whether it is just a modern folk tale passed around and augmented by whoever picks it up, is really secondary. But it is significant in that it represents a certain mindset which seems willing to accept any fact or example, as long as it is "scientific," to prove a point. (One source attributes a similar experiment to a Mrs. Dorothy Retallack, a housewife from Denver, Colorado, who could kill her houseplants in four weeks with a steady diet of Led Zeppelin and Vanilla Fudge.)

The implications of the plant plot test are to make us think, "If rock music can do that to plants, just imagine what it does to people!" However, even assuming the test was real, the results tell nothing about human beings. It says nothing in particular about plants either. A careful scientist would never draw such an analogy or allow such a vaguely constructed test to answer hard questions.

Music *does* affect people. Musicians and their audiences have always known this. Long before rock came along, doctors were studying the uses of music in treating people physically and psychologically. They found that music played in factories could help people work more efficiently, that mental patients slept better and fought with each other less when music was played over the public address system. Today's supermarkets, dentists' offices, airline terminals and elevators all have their own brand of music for their own therapeutic purposes. Dentists play soothing music to help calm people's fears; supermarkets hope to create a cheerful atmosphere where people feel good about shopping.

In fact, the emotional influence of music has been carefully documented in tests conducted by psychologists in the early 1930s. A psychologist named Hevener explored the whole spectrum of human emotion from joyous, playful and aggressive, to mournful, yearning and depressing —using classical music entirely. She found that even people untrained in music could intelligently and accurately describe their feelings as they listened to various pieces of music.

Other psychologists and musicologists devised a number of tests to determine the physical and emotional sensitivity of listeners to music, and their awareness of its effects on them. The research found that while people were quite sensitive, they were also quite aware of what the music was doing to them emotionally. They were, if asked, able to give quite detailed and objective statements about their feelings. In other words, although people were emotionally influenced by music, they were not dominated by it. Their feelings were always monitored by the mind. Those listening knew what they were feeling; they were not influenced without knowing it.[1]

Objective research challenges the notion that rock seizes a person's mind or otherwise takes control, a notion which Bob Larson epitomized when he stated, "It is quite obvious to any qualified, objective observer that teenagers dancing to rock music often enter hypnotic trances. When control of the mind is weakened or lost, evil influences can often take possession. Loss of self-control is dangerous and sinful. In a state of hypnosis the mind of the listener can respond to almost any suggestion given to it."[2]

Is rock hypnotic? Let's first try to understand what true hypnosis is. The notions of loss of control and zombielike trances are popular misconceptions played up by Hollywood and stage hypnotists, but far removed from the real thing. Dr. William Kroger, a pioneer in the use of clinical hypnosis in medical therapy, has for over forty years taught the basic principles of hypnosis to more than one hundred thousand physicians throughout the world. He describes hypnosis as simply a process of relaxation, "whereby, because you relax better, you hear better. And whenever you hear better, whatever I say to you or whatever you say to yourself will 'sink in' better. If it sinks in better, you will respond better. This allows greater awareness. Since you are more aware, you naturally cannot be asleep. You go into a superalert state whenever you desire and you come out of it whenever you wish. You are always in control."[3]

Hypnosis is seen as a state of alert concentration involving relaxation. Hypnotized people are fully aware and in control of themselves and their thoughts at all time. They have *more* control, not less.

Concentration. Relaxation. Two postures difficult to create or maintain at a rock concert. And what of this extreme vulnerability to suggestion which has been described? Even stage magicians know that subjects under hypnosis cannot be made to do anything against their own will. Thus, people do not become mindless

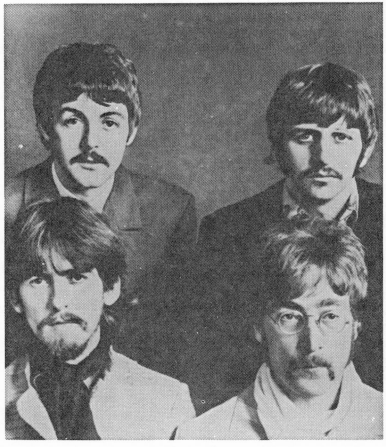

The Beatles

zombies, whether responding to a hypnotist's suggestion or in subjection to the so-called hypnotic powers of rock music.

But looking at the way people jump around at rock concerts, one might think it was the music whipping everyone into a frenzy. It is a logical assumption. However, it is one which must be discarded in light of better information. People jump and gyrate, leap around and lose control because they *want* to. Rock frenzies are self-induced, not rhythm induced, and each listener can choose how to react. Music does have power to move, but not to override normal sensibilities.

It is ironic that what made people scream and faint in the sixties fails to elicit anything but a snicker today. Watch a film of the Beatles at Shea Stadium, the stands packed with thousands of screeching, crying fans, and you wonder what all the commotion was about. Was it the music? No. If music was the mover, the beat would still drive people crazy. Put on a stack of old Beatle records and you won't get anybody to scream and jump around now. It's out of style. They don't *want* to do it.

Invasion of the Body Snatchers

With no new ground to break in the area of music's effects upon emotions, researchers and critics turned their attention to the body to see how it was being affected by the potent strains of rock. If you have ever walked out onto a disco dance floor unprepared, you might think the music was getting everybody all excited. The sound system blasts away at people jammed hip to hip and toe to toe, arms and legs flailing like disconnected puppets amidst flashing colored lights and fog machines churning the atmosphere into soup. As the electronic music drones on and on, people try to outdo each other in more outrageous

67

dances. The superenergized scene grinds away for hours.

Some would say this is because people cannot help themselves. Again, Larson sums it up when he says, "Often the muscular reaction to music is an involuntary action requiring conscious muscular restraint to cease the action. It is this principle that gives the rock beat its irresistible urge. This is only a partial explanation as to where teenagers get such tremendous amounts of energy to do those frantic dances for extended periods of time."[4]

He suggests that rock music somehow takes control of the muscles and acts as an energy transfusion, pushing listeners to wilder heights and physical gyrations beyond their normal ability.

Dr. John Diamond, an Australian psychiatrist, believes, however, that rock music can considerably *reduce* a person's capacity for jumping around. He says that listening to rock music makes one physically weaker, depending on the beat. In an article in the *Los Angeles Times,* Diamond's theory is explained, indicating that "more than 90% of the hundreds of people . . . tested on an electronic strain gauge have registered instantaneous loss of 2/3 of their normal muscle strength," when subjected to certain rock songs.[5]

That doesn't speak well for extended periods of gyrating. Any frenzy whipped up would be a feeble frenzy, indeed. Actually, about all Diamond really shows is that almost anything can be proven with a few meters and gauges. The effects of rock on the body are best concluded to be uncertain—with one exception. Everyone agrees that loud sounds of any type (jet engines, subways, explosions, loud music) hurt the ears. Prolonged exposure to loud sound sometimes damages hearing permanently. But ear damage has to do with sound waves, not style. As for rock rhythms affecting the rest of the body, the proof of

68

harm remains to be seen.

We know: (1) syncopation is a common musical device used in a variety of musical styles with no particularly abnormal effects on people; (2) all music affects people emotionally but does not short-circuit the normal mental processes; and, thus (3) rock music is not hypnotic. Any apparent loss of control is self-induced by enthusiastic listeners and limited to the immediate popularity of the performer or the atmosphere surrounding the performance. People are not emotionally or psychologically damaged by exposure to rock beats and are not seized or overpowered by rock rhythms against their will.

A beat or rhythm is not evil. The very fact that rhythm is a universal part of all existence should show us that it is a natural part of our lives and not something to be feared or condemned. Rock may use stronger or more urgent rhythms than other forms of music, but since all music uses rhythm, the issue becomes a question of degree or intensity.

Some suggest that when the beat becomes the main focus of the music, overwhelming all other components, that is when the trouble begins. The pulsating beat assaults the mind and puts it to sleep, so to speak, opening it to evil invasion while the listener is off guard. That is the assertion. But how is such a statement to be proven? Or disproven? The argument at that point moves from the realm of the concrete to the metaphysical. And metaphysical arguments cannot be settled in the laboratory.

While it may be possible to show that under certain conditions the mind may enter an altered state of consciousness, does it necessarily follow that evil forces automatically invade when normal attention is diminished or changed? On what grounds is that to be believed? The point is that the interplay between the physical, mental, emotional and spiritual aspects of human beings are extremely complex and not likely to be neatly elucidated by any single system of study or thought, even a religious one. Much more careful study and research is necessary before any concrete conclusions can be reached.

Help Me, Dr. Feelgood!

No, rock music cannot take you anywhere you do not want to go. However, it can make it easy for you to go somewhere you do want to go but know you shouldn't. This, of course, has nothing to do with rhythm, beat, hypnosis or anything else. Instead, this "grease on the slide to depravity" is supplied by the cultural atmosphere surrounding rock music—the way the fans and the performers themselves live.

Rock is seen as a Dr. Feelgood, the light-hearted healing agent that slaps Band-Aids on the various emotional bruises of its fans. This is one of rock's most attractive and influential guises, seemingly harmless on the surface. But isn't there more to it than that?

6

THE MAKING OF A MORAL DILEMMA

A WAVE OF VULGAR, FILTHY and suggestive music has inundated the land. . . . It is artistically and morally depressing and should be suppressed by press and pulpit."[1]

This apt scrap of journalistic judgment is a sticky label that reflects a common view about rock music. However, the above snippet came from a magazine called the *Musical Courier,* and the music which so outraged the writer was a slick, fast-paced, jumpy music called ragtime—now nostalgically remembered in records and movies like *The Sting.* The year was 1899 and ragtime was the rage, and by most accounts the state of the union was morally bankrupt.

Morality, it seems, is always taking it on the chin in America. Often, music is labeled a prime undermining factor.

How Low Can You Go?

Problem: Rock music is a rough music, dealing with the lower side of human nature. It creates an unhealthy mental environment for its listeners through suggestive lyrics and obscene connotations. Rock excites a person's sexual drives, and projects an atmosphere where immorality is acceptable.

It seems a curious fact of history that each new generation thinks itself the first and the older generation thinks it the worst. Of course, it is neither. History is crowded with examples where certain graybeards have shaken their heads, predicting the downfall of the world over this or that newfangled invention. And the steady erosion of morality at the hands of popular entertainers is a time-worn theme.

This is a universal trend noted by John Rublowsky in his book *Popular Music*. "It is hard to believe that the waltz was considered scandalous when it was first introduced at the end of the eighteenth century." Polite society refused to condone such a barbaric dance. Their music was the minuet, much more "refined." But despite prevailing opinion, "the minuet was replaced and the waltz became respectable."[2]

Years later, jazz was named as the cause of horrendous moral lapses. *Ladies Home Journal* put the question like this: "Does Jazz Put the Sin in Syncopation?" and also championed the cry, "Unspeakable Jazz Must Go!" Some anonymous busybody traced the moral decline and fall of a thousand girls in Chicago from 1920 to 1922 directly to jazz. Women were reported to leap onto tables and tear off their clothes while screaming in ecstasy as the Original Dixieland Jazz Band raced through its paces. America's youth were thought to be in serious peril from the creeping menace of jazz.

72

Twenty years later it was a new peril and the menace was named Frankie, as in Sinatra. "Swoonatraism" was sweeping the country, especially among bobby-soxed females aged fourteen. "His cigarette butts, his un-eaten cornflakes became highly prized items. So did locks of his hair, often plucked from his very head. The hysteria was compared to the Children's Crusade of the Middle Ages."[3]

The wheels of style revolve slowly onward, changing with the times. However, certain themes remain the same: sex is a perennial.

Sex in song is not new. Every age has had its bawdy songs, illicit lyrics, double meanings. Rock music is no exception. And from this point of view, it stands guilty; sexuality of all kinds is expressed in rock music. Popular music, including rock, has a way of expressing what is on the minds of its writers and listeners, the basic thoughts and feelings of human beings. When people have sex on their minds, it comes out in a song.

Most popular songs (of any era) are of the boy-meets/loses/marries-girl type; innocent, sugar-coated, inoffensive sentiments. Rock has this side, but often its expressions are stronger, earthier; it is a forceful music, and the words it chooses are forceful, too.

It could be argued that there is more blatant sexual immorality being peddled in popular music now than ever before; I believe this is true. There is also more explicit sexuality displayed in movies, books, television and magazines as part of the growing permissiveness of American society.

I would suggest that music, although clearly part of the "too much sex" problem, is *not* the cause. The problem of too much sex in media is much bigger than rock music itself. That does not excuse rock for its part in the mess, but it should clue critics to the fact that burning piles of

73

rock records in church parking lots will not solve the problem.

Like television shows and movies which rely heavily on sex to sell themselves, music that indulges itself in the same way should be suppressed. But should all rock music be banned because of the excesses of some songs? That is hardly fair. Rock is very complex; not all lyrics to rock songs speak about sex, and not all sexually explicit songs are in the rock style. The problem of too much sex is bigger than simply sexy lyrics in rock tunes.

An example can be found in the field of country music.

Country Crude

Some say country music came out of the Tennessee hills with Mother Maybelle Carter who, with her family, played the simple songs of the country folk that had been passed around for so long nobody knew where they came from. She was joined by others who sought to preserve a distinct musical heritage largely ignored or forgotten by modern city dwellers.

The music was open-handed and honest, simple, even crude in its construction. It was songs about the land, about people, about good times and bad, about life as many lived it. It was played on basic instruments, often homemade, shaped to the skills of musicians who had no formal musical training and most likely no formal schooling of any kind. Folk music. Music from the heart of the country, and from the hearts of the country folk.

But over the years country music changed. Today, the deep-rooted, prosaic mainstay of millions of Americans is progressively treating themes which at one time would have been considered taboo.

An article in *Billboard* magazine (the music industry's top trade journal) examined the lyric content of recent country chart-toppers and noted that while "famous for its self-preoccupation with cheating, drinking and good-women-gone-bad themes, country music now appears to have discovered modern day vices with new glee. Drugs are turning up in country songs with surprising frequency, along with frank references to sex, physical situations and political events."[4]

The titles of the songs themselves leave no doubt where the message is headed. Here is a random sampling: "Bombed, Boozed and Busted," by Joe Sun; "Cocain Train," by Johnny Paycheck; "Put Your Clothes Back On," by Joe Stampley; "While I was Making Love to You," by Susie Allanson; "If I Said You Had a Beautiful Body, Would You Hold it Against Me," a smash hit by the Bellamy Brothers; "Caffeine, Nicotine and Benzedrine (And Wish Me Lucky)," by Jerry Reed.

Are these isolated examples? No. As country music increases in popularity, its expressions become more suggestive. "The Coward of the County," by Kenny Rogers is a notable example. It is a simple ballad about violence and revenge; the refrain informs listeners that "sometimes you have to fight to be a man." But the focus of the song is, for lack of a more polite term, a gang rape (for which the villains in the song are beaten bloody by the once-cowardly hero).

Was anyone shocked by this? Apparently not. "The Coward of the County" rocketed to the top of the country charts and then crossed over onto the pop charts and climbed all the way to the top there, too. For his part, Kenny Rogers has been confirmed as country music's entertainer of the year for two years running, has won numerous Grammy Awards, and appears on television regularly (where he occasionally performs "Coward"). Yet there was no squawk raised over the song or its slimy subject.

76

Perhaps the lack of strong reaction against country music's new permissiveness is due to ambiguity; maybe people do not understand what the songs are really saying. No, in fact, the opposite is more likely. People understand quite well what is being said. The *Billboard* article pinpoints a very disturbing fact: the lyrics of country songs are much more accessible than other kinds of music. "Unlike rock 'n' roll—where studio arrangement, instrumental flamboyance and technical wizardry take priority over the words—country music is founded, formed and fashioned on the strengths of its lyrics. . . . Unquestionably, lyrics count as the single most important ingredient in a country hit."[5]

For anyone who finds this unsettling, Charlie Monk, head of April-Blackwood, one of the largest country music publishing houses, offered this defense: "Sure, there's more profanity in country music these days. But then country lyrics have always intimated sex and promiscuous affairs. The backstreets to romance have always been a part of country music." The *Billboard* article concludes: "The general feeling among country music executives is that as country music comes of age, it is continuing to do what it's always done best: reflect the times."[6]

Rock and the Vigilantes

Suppose for a moment that a group of vigilantes were to rise up and take it upon themselves to rid society of media that exploit raunchy material. Rock, of course, would be among the first to go. But to be thorough and consistent this group would have to go to bat against television, magazines of all types (not just the raunchy ones), advertisements in all mediums, movies and books of all types. Johnny Carson dishes out crude, suggestive jokes to millions of people every evening—is anyone protesting? To

77

reform all the areas mentioned would be a Herculean task, indeed. But suppose they were able to clean them all up. Then what?

Consider the classics. *Oedipus the King,* one of the most widely read of the classic Greek plays, centers around the dual theme of incest and murder. Homer's brave Odysseus played the crafty culprit of a host of crimes ranging from fornication to thievery to murder. Oedipus and Odysseus are introduced to students in the eighth grade in many school systems.

And what about classical music? Perhaps because classical music's image is propriety itself in a stiff white shirt and black tuxedo, most would not think of moving in to reform it in any way. In fact, classical music is often suggested as an antidote to rock music. Yet classical music, especially opera, often deals in rank immorality. Murder, adultery, rape, promiscuity, revenge, graft, corruption in high places are all part of the operatic tradition.

Die Fledermaus, by Johann Strauss, one of the best-loved comic operas, is the story of lover-swapping singles. The action takes place at a ball given by homosexual Prince Orlovsky whose main aria invites his guests to make love, "each to his own taste." It sounds more like the plot of an X-rated movie than a genteel nineteenth-century work of art.

Wagner, universally recognized as one of the world's truly great composers, was a megalomaniac within reach of lunacy. He was grossly immoral, selfish, adulterous, arrogant, wildly hedonistic and violently racist. He was a thief to boot. Yet, Wagner's works are performed today throughout the major concert venues of the world. There seems to be little concern that they were composed by a man of unquestionably immoral character.

In a new book on classical music released by a Christian

publisher, an entire section devoted to Wagner unbelievably manages to downplay the evil this man represented. With a bare hint at the truth, the book innocently mentions that Wagner was "inconsiderate, self-obsessed, and melancholy."[7] And this was a man rabidly anti-Christian and anti-Jewish, much admired by Hitler, who found in Wagner a kindred spirit and in his music a way to stoke the German war machine.

Classical music has much that would condemn it from a strictly moral standpoint, whether in the lyrics or in the lives of its composers. To consign offensive classical recordings to the flames with the rest would strike most of us as barbaric. We are raised to regard classical music as the highest expression of musical art. Burning a few rock records, on the other hand, seems like an appropriate demonstration despite the fact that the contents of any random rock record may actually be less offensive than the typical opera.

In presenting the inconsistencies of our culture in its thinking about classical music and the casual tolerance of immorality in many other forms, my purpose is not to condone rock music's excesses or defend them in any way. I am not saying immorality in music is right because it is accepted or that because we accept immorality in many other areas of our lives, we should accept it in rock music as well. My purpose has been to put the problem into perspective.

Burning classical records or refusing to listen to Wagner because of his corrupt life is absurd—just as burning rock records is absurd. Plainly, the problem is not so much the perception of immorality as music appreciation. The classical music buff is not long bothered that Wagner hated Jews, indulged in orgies or stole the wife of his conductor. Wagner's music is still appreciated for what it is.

79

The question of music appreciation, as we have seen, is a matter of culture and taste. We grow up accepting classical music and think highly of it (whether we actually understand or listen to it) because our culture assures us it is worthy. The cultural trend toward the acceptance of rock as a legitimate artistic style is just beginning. Will rock ever hold the same high regard reserved for the classical arts? Time alone will tell.

Tunnel Vision

Rock is often characterized as expressing only sex-, drug- or anarchy-related themes. While it is true that there have been plenty of rock songs grouped around those themes, the music is much more complex than that.

Rock music is thematically complex, and the fact can be simply demonstrated by looking at a popular song chart. Among the typical boy/girl romantic musings are songs which explore basic human sentiments (loneliness, vulnerability, genuine love or the absence of it), modern concerns (the emptiness of transitory relationships, the drive for success, facing old age and world peace) and how to live (adopting simpler living patterns, getting back to basics, the brutality of urban street life).

These would be among the positive expressions which rock music voices. There are also negative ideas expressed in rock that are far more serious than the issues of sex and drugs. Yet these themes receive little attention.

Rock music is an active proponent of two of this century's most ruthless and damaging philosophies: secular humanism and nihilism. Briefly stated, secular humanism is that branch of thought which asserts the dignity and worth of humanity and its capacity for self-realization through reason alone, rejecting any supernatural or spiritual considerations. Nihilism asserts the dismal view

80

that traditional values, morals and beliefs are unfounded, that society's present condition is so irredeemably hopeless that annihilation may be preferable to any positive attempt to save it. After all, existence is meaningless anyway.

Secular humanism is the darling of the moment; almost all modern literature, drama, movies, music espouse the view consciously or unconsciously that "man is all we've got." The heros of stage and story are trotted before us to face inhuman obstacles, often with supreme courage, unshakeable conviction and self-sacrificing love—all without a mention that we might draw strength from our Creator or that we even *have* a spiritual side. This is insidious, subtle and damning.

Ultimately, secular humanism leads to nihilism because myopic good faith cannot forever withstand the terrible onslaught of reality: we are lost without God! Lost in every sense of the word. When the humanists realize this they throw themselves into the bottomless pit of eternal despair, despair which can harden into nihilism. For, after denying spiritual needs, and never admitting God's presence, from where is salvation to come?

Of course, this is rarely presented overtly; the hint is usually much more subtle. But when was the last time you watched a television program, even a "family" program, which remotely suggested that the character's problems might have spiritual solutions or that the hero may at some later date be haunted by the moral implications of his actions?

Here is the real dilemma of the modern age, not sex, drugs or rebellion. Those are merely blemishes, the symptoms of a raging, deadly disease. To treat the symptoms without properly diagnosing the disease is to flail away uselessly.

The disease is real. It has touched the very core of life on this planet and now everything suffers—the way we think, the way we act, our relationships, the books we read, the music we listen to. The disease has contaminated everything of value. Rock music is just one more avenue of human endeavor which has been contaminated by too close contact with the disease of secular humanism. The cure does not lie in banning all contaminated avenues, be they rock or literature or theater. The disease will still remain. The cure lies in combating the disease directly. This is the topic of part two.

PART II
MAGIC IN THE MUSIC

7

YOU AND ME AGAINST THE WORLD

ONE OF THE CONSTANT struggles of a young rock group is finding a place to practice. With various bands I have practiced in garages, basements, a condemned gymnasium, a converted root cellar and a church. It is not every church that will let a rock group wail within its walls, but this particular church took a special interest in us as musicians with a problem (no place to store our expensive equipment or practice) and helped out.

I was sitting alone in front of my amplifier one afternoon just before our practice session was to start when the minister's wife came into the room. She listened for a short while and walked over to me. "You play beautifully," she said.

"Thanks," I said, a little embarrassed. I wasn't used to

my guitar noises being called "beautiful."

"You know, you really should think about using your talent for the Lord." She was very serious. I didn't know what to say. She went on and told me how great it would be if I dedicated my music to serving God and reaching other young people for him. A commendable idea, I thought, but she had no idea what she was saying.

Although I listened politely, I knew there was no way to do what she suggested, no practical way on earth at that time. The reason was simple: the church would not accept the kind of music I played; it was too loud and raucous. What the minister's wife had in mind was something softer, more traditional, only played with guitar, thus making it upbeat. If I played that kind of music, which she and the church would like, nobody I knew (none of my friends, at least) would want to listen to it. And I wouldn't want to play it.

At that time, contemporary Christian music was at an awkward stage, not satisfied with the traditional fare, yet not ready to rock. Groups that tried to push the limits, using rock to put across the Christian message, wound up getting shut down or driven underground for their efforts.

But things were beginning to change; a new spirit was awakening people to the possibilities of joining the power of rock to the powerful message of Jesus.

Mixing Rock and Religion

So far in this book, we have been examining some of the controversies orbiting rock 'n' roll. My aim has not been to justify all the bad in rock, excuse it or explain away its faults. Instead, I have tried to offer some perspective on the problem, answer some of the major objections and show that there is nothing intrinsically wrong with rock as a style of music.

86

Once I was telling Mike, my friend from Mother Rush days, that I was working on a book about rock music. He was interested, so I outlined it for him. He listened quietly and then, with a grin, summed up what I was saying. "It's kind of like trying to defend a mode of transportation that's being exploited by bandits. There's nothing immoral about transportation, but the bandits have a way of corrupting everything they touch." That is what has happened to rock, in a way. Bandits have all but ruined the vehicle of rock for a lot of people.

Yet, if rock is a wreck, I think it can be salvaged and even put to good use. J. G. Machen, in *Christianity and Culture,* suggests that "the Christian cannot be satisfied as long as any human activity is either opposed to Christianity or out of all connection with Christianity. . . . The Christian, therefore, cannot be indifferent to any branch of human endeavor. It must be brought into some relationship with the gospel."[1]

Many Christian musicians feel the same way. They are starting to put rock music to use for Christian entertainment, praise and worship, and for spreading the good news about Jesus Christ. Here is the cure for the nihilism and secular humanism afflicting popular music. Yet for many the cure seems as bad as the disease. Rock and religion do not seem to mix.

This chapter and the ones following will look at rock music from a Christian point of view, and examine the problems Christians struggle with when they come into contact with this thing called Jesus Rock.

Turn Your Radio On

It was 5:30 on a typical Chicago afternoon when I was trucking down the freeway, fleeing through the rush-hour traffic to the suburbs. Like most rush-hour drivers, I had

87

one hand on the steering wheel and the other on the knob of my car radio, trying to tune in some companionship for the long ride home.

The skinny red finger on the radio dial slid across the FM band and stopped momentarily. I caught the tail of a song fading into the air. A supercharged, nonstop deejay with a voice smooth as spun butter then said, "This is the all new FM 92, your Christian Alternative. Now, turning to our spiffy sports corner . . ." What's this? My Christian alternative? I was a lucky winner in the game known as radio roulette. I had stumbled on a rare animal in the FM/AM jungle of airwaves: a contemporary Christian radio station that is upfront, professional and plays a solid format of contemporary Christian music.

If you were an idle player of radio roulette, spinning the dial and tuning in a station like FM 92, you would perhaps notice nothing out of the ordinary—upbeat music hosted by golden-throated deejays. Pretty standard fare, on the surface, until you listened more closely. They were talking about Jesus!

Too Close for Comfort

Problem: Rock music is worldly music. As Christians we are called out of the world to live a spiritual life. When we imitate the world's music and use the world's gimmicks, we are directly disobeying the Bible's command to be separate from the world.

Christians in all places and times have had trouble figuring out, let alone agreeing on, how much of this world it is safe to participate in.

During the Middle Ages many groups formed independent communities, or monasteries, which were totally self-sufficient so that their members would not have to come into contact with the world which they considered

88

evil. Other groups were not so fussy; declining complete separation, they merely adopted a different style of dress, or different eating habits—anything that would help to remind them that they were not of the world.

Nowadays, Christians look pretty much like anybody else, and they do not live by themselves in walled cities. But various religious groups still make rules to prescribe acceptable levels of worldly contact. Every group seems to have laid down its own guidelines about fashions, customs, work, eating habits and any other aspect of living in the world. Music, since it is so much a part of this world, is often called into question.

From the beginning rock has been on the outs with organized religion. But when Christian musicians began picking up the rock style for use in Christian services and records, the pot really started to boil. To many, the sounds coming out of supposedly Christian records and radio stations are alarmingly similar to the sounds which they fight so hard to keep out of their homes. Except for the words, you often cannot tell them apart. It appears suspiciously that Christian music is being contaminated by contact with worldly rock music. Apparently, there is something wrong here . . . isn't there?

Talk to the Jock
To further explore the problem I paid a visit to that supercharged deejay whose voice I had heard on the freeway. His name is Rick Patton, and he is program director for radio station WYCA, Hammond, Indiana. Here is his side of the story:

"When I became a Christian, I came off a fifteen-year high as a popular disc jockey—beautiful music, rock 'n' roll, country, talk shows, public appearances—I'd done it all in various stations around the country. I came to

89

WYCA as a brand new Christian, thinking, 'This is just exactly what I want to do.' I wanted to work for God as hard as I knew how and was grateful for the chance to do it.

"Well, my first day on the air, I opened up the microphone and blasted away, doing what I normally do in a very powerful way. In a matter of minutes the phones went bananas. Lights were flashing everywhere, phone circuits overloaded. People were calling in, 'You can't be saved. The way you talk . . . ' We started receiving letters saying, 'Who is this madman?' People were offended by the way I worked a radio show.

"But the music hadn't changed. I was putting more zip into the patter between songs, but we were still playing very traditional, what they call inspirational music—the kind of music religious stations have been playing for years and years. And at night I'd drive home from work, listening to the station, and I'd feel hunger pangs. The music the station programmed left me empty; I wasn't being satisfied. I felt cheated as a disc jockey; people out there without God needed to hear about him, and I wasn't being given a chance to reach them. All the things I'd learned as a professional were being wasted. I began to feel that maybe I had made a mistake in coming to a religious radio station.

"As the weeks passed I got into the habit of not listening to the station at all because it was beginning to depress me. Instead, I'd listen to some of Chicago's top rock stations—tight, professional, with-it stations. I prayed, 'God, why can't we have a station like this? A station that would play Christian music that I can understand, that can lift my spirit, speak to me? Why not, God?'

"I didn't realize that this kind of Christian music did exist. One day soon after that, I was dropping a record on the turntable; I inadvertently put the needle down on a

90

song called 'What Good's It Gonna Do You?' by the Pat Terry Group. The song had a little kick to it, with a slight rock beat and a style that I was used to. I said to myself, 'Hey, that's good! Why can't we play that?' I played it. No reaction. Working up a little more courage, I started dropping the needle on other records we had laying around and discovered a lot of good material that wasn't being played.

"Oddly, the message they put across was exactly the same as the more traditional religious music. It was just in a different package. I started seeking out these new performers, attending concerts, buying records, getting in touch with what was going on. I saw a whole new world of music opening up before me.

"If this is where people are, I reasoned, this is where we need to be. I started formulating plans for a top-notch contemporary Christian rock format. I took my ideas to the station's owners, and after deliberating for a month they gave me the go-ahead. I became the station's program director.

"The battle was on.

"The first day of the new format the phones rang off the hook. The heat I'd experienced when I first signed on the air was a cool breeze compared to the flames that shot up this time. Angry letters came in by the hundreds every week. Someone wrote in, 'The Devil has taken over WYCA; he's firmly entrenched there in the person of Rick Patton!' The thing that got me was that people would say they're telling me these things out of love, and then WHAM!—let me have it.

"I spent a lot of time in prayer those few months, questioning. Is this right? Is this God's will?

"I hung on a few more weeks, and then began to notice a change in the letters and phone calls. The tide was turn-

91

ing; people were coming out in support for our new format. A controversy had been created, and now the backlash was forming that would sweep away the opposition. Inside of six months we received over thirteen hundred letters, and almost all of them were in support of our new format.

"We've come a long way since then. I've seen the station blossom as it reaches people like never before. There is an excitement here that something is happening, something has come to life after being dead so long.

"I came out of the world after being a disc jockey for fifteen years and working in a lot of professional markets where you can't be sloppy or second-rate. You have to have some type of an impact or they'll just shoot you out of your chair. When I came to WYCA as a Christian, all I could do was to give back to God as much talent as he had given me; otherwise, I'd be cheating him. I got accused of being a non-Christian, an unbeliever, unsaved and all the rest because I did not sound like the average Christian radio personality. The reason people take offense, I believe, is that many Christians misinterpret professionalism for worldliness.

"Because a person is a professional, talented, skillful and representing the highest standards of his profession, does not mean that he is worldly. To ask that person to perform at a level less than is measured by the talent that has been given to him by God is unjust and unfair. There is a definite need for Christian rock music that can reach the people who turn off the more traditional approach. Rock has the ability to arrest a listener; nail him down long enough for him to hear what the message has to say. But no one is going to listen if we are satisfied with putting out anything that is less than the very best."

Recently, contemporary Christian music has responded to the need for a strong commitment to quality in all phases—performing, recording and production. But that does not mean the music has grown worldly. The music industry has developed certain standards of quality over the years. There is nothing wrong with using those standards to carry the Christian message. In fact, if communication is our goal, achieving the highest professional standards is imperative.

Pharisees and Weaker Brothers

Reaching people with the Christian message through music is possible only if the music reaches them. This means more, however, than just seeing that Christian records are placed in the hands of people who want to listen. It also means taking the message to people in a form they can understand. That cannot happen as long as Christians maintain what has been called a fortress mentality, us against them.

The fortress mentality is a subtle trap which many Christians fall into unknowingly. We retreat into ourselves because we fear becoming worldly. We erect a fortress around ourselves to keep the secular, or worldly, element from contaminating us. The world is seen as an enemy to be battled or retreated from. The main danger with this kind of thinking is that in keeping away from the world, we also remain isolated from the world's people who need the love, forgiveness and compassion only Christians can offer in the message of Jesus Christ.

True enough, the Bible does warn Christians on many occasions to keep free of worldly entanglements. But when the Bible speaks of worldliness, it is talking about falling into the world's sins and way of thinking. It is letting something take God's place in our lives. Worldliness is not mere contact with the world's people, places and things.

Jesus, in fact, explained that Christians were to remain

93

in the world as an example to others. Jesus identified his enemy, and ours: the evil one. When he prayed for those who would come after him, Jesus said, "I pray thee, not to take them out of the world, but to keep them from the evil one" (Jn 17:15 NEB). He called us salt. Salt preserves and protects; it has a good influence. And as someone once pointed out, salt does not do any good unless it is sprinkled around. And it cannot get sprinkled around if it stays in the shaker.

When the apostle Paul warns "do not be conformed to this world" (Rom 12:2), he is talking more about character than conduct. Limiting our participation in society is not his aim. He is more concerned about what kind of people we *are,* not how we dress, what we eat, whether we have non-Christian friends or listen to rock music. An unnatural fear of becoming worldly or a preoccupation with figuring out what is or is not worldly is a telltale sign of the fortress mentality.

The fortress mentality is not a new problem; people in Jesus' day had trouble with it, too. Of all the groups Jesus came into contact with, two stand out in this regard: the Pharisees and, for lack of a better term, the weaker brothers.

The weaker brothers were those whose faith was weak, who often stumbled and wavered in trying to carry out all that the Jewish law demanded. Although sincere, the weaker brothers were easily tempted and in constant need of repentance and reassurance. For them, religion was a struggle. Jesus had a great deal of sympathy for this group. He wanted to free them from the law's demands so they could establish personal contact with God.

The Pharisees were the superstars of Judaism. They knew the law forward and backward; they had faith to burn. Pharisees maintained a fanatical attention to de-

94

tail, always weighing, judging and debating every action and consequence. In devotion and ambition, the Pharisees were second to none. They were the most religious people of the day, without question.

Yet, of all people, the Pharisees earned Jesus' harshest criticism. They made their religion a wall, with themselves on one side and everyone else on the other. They avoided contact with anyone who was not like them. Their fastidiousness led them to condemn the lesser faith of others. Since no one could outdo them, they placed themselves as the final authority on all religious matters, making themselves judges over all. The Pharisees reinforced the already cumbersome Jewish law with hundreds of minute rules and regulations which prescribed exacting performance in every conceivable situation, thus further alienating their kinsmen from salvation. In time, as a result of their fortress mentality, they developed a kind of superiority complex which effectively stated, "We're right and everyone else is wrong."

Of course, the Pharisees did not see anything amiss in the way they lived. They thought of themselves as sincere, devoted Jews, doing only what God required. So thick had the walls grown that they no longer heard the cries from the other side. Ultimately, their fortress mentality led them to reject and murder God's own Son. This they did so their religion would not be corrupted with the "worldly" ideas which Jesus taught. The Pharisees had become more spiritual than God.

We still have the Pharisees and weaker brothers with us today. There are those who find rock music a stumbling block to their faith. Often these are new Christians whose old life is still painfully close. Rock only reminds them of how they used to live. Like many new Christians, they want a dramatic outward change to go with their new in-

95

ward change.

I have talked with people who have told me similar stories: "When I first became a Christian I threw out all my rock albums. I couldn't bear to listen to them." There is then a pause to reflect, and a rueful smile. "Now, I just wish I had them back!" It is not that the person is any less a Christian than before; on the contrary, he or she has become strong enough to once again enjoy the music without the negative associations. Of course, we should be careful of and sympathetic toward our weaker brothers, as Jesus was. Rock may not be for everyone; some, like recent converts, may not be able to handle it until they achieve a degree of maturity and some distance from their old life.

The apostle Paul speaks directly to this issue in the fourteenth and fifteenth chapters of Romans. However, for his day the problem was not music but whether or not to drink wine, celebrate traditional holidays or eat meat which had been offered to idols in pagan ceremonies. In essence, Paul's conclusion was that people have to decide questions of this nature for themselves, according to their own consciences and circumstances. He elaborates to say that weaker brothers must be cared for. The strong must protect the weak. If, at a certain time or place, playing or listening to rock music may cause a weaker brother to stumble, then we are to refrain. Otherwise, we are free to do as we please.

Paul also has a few words to say to the weaker brothers: they are not to reproach those stronger than themselves, or find fault with their behavior. The stronger brother is not responsible to the weaker for his actions; he is responsible only to God. This is important. Too often, I think, those who call themselves weaker brothers are really Pharisees. Outwardly, they may seem humble as they dutifully struggle through life. But inwardly, they pride

96

themselves on their abstinence from things they consider worldly. Worse, they try to impose the same restrictions on others on the grounds that, "Remember the weaker brother; you shouldn't cause him to stumble." Of course, the weaker brother is imaginary, they have no real person in mind at all. The Pharisee is only using the idea of a weaker brother to force compliance with his petty rules. We should recognize that deception for what it is.

Jesus' criticism of the Pharisees and his compassion for the weaker brothers helps us deal with the problem of worldliness and rock music. The differences between Jesus' and the Pharisees' style of reaching people is plain. Jesus did not mind being seen with ordinary people. He went wherever he had to go to be heard, even to the homes of thieves and worse. It was the religious leaders who would have nothing to do with sinners. Jesus knew he had nothing to fear from the world; it held no seductive power over him. He was free to take his message anywhere, using any form of communication available for his purpose. He wants us to follow his example.

Rock music has that ability to reach many people where they live. Coupled with the Christian message it becomes a very powerful form of communication—more powerful than many traditional forms since some people turn off such approaches. Being powerful and new in its approach does not make the music worldly.

Trade in Your Old Vehicle
Actually, our notions of what is and is not worldly are relative and limited to our own peculiar cultural biases. And even those notions are subject to change without our notice. Thurlow Spurr, musical director for the PTL Network, director of the Festival of Praise touring choir and long-time leader of the traveling musical group, the

97

Spurrlows, relates this story.

A lady came to me in the studio after a PTL Club television program. The orchestra and singers had just done a very new song that was, let's say, "strong."

She said, "What you did today was okay, but you know, I have one of your old records and I like the more conservative music on it better."

What she didn't know was that fifteen years ago, some of our concerts were promptly canceled by churches and even youth organizations when that particular record was released because that music was too "worldly." One of the nation's best-known major religious radio stations banned that record and instructed their deejays not to play any of our music. Not only had we contaminated sacred music, they thought, but our music had also contaminated us!

Well, thank God, things have changed! Most people have discovered that music is only the vehicle to convey a message. The vehicle can change. . . . And God help us if it doesn't![2]

Spurr has touched on a very potent problem but one seldom addressed, the problem of religious censorship. Often, religious leaders find themselves in the position of censoring what their audiences will be allowed to hear—for fear of losing their audience's support. For example, a radio programmer might say, "If I play this record, people might get upset and stop listening to my station." Many leaders will privately admit Christian rock is okay, yet will not publicly endorse it because of financial reasons ("My station will lose listeners") or political motives ("My church board won't like it"). This is worldliness! Sacrificing spiritual considerations for financial or political motives!

Christian musicians and disc jockeys are finding the rock form to be a most useful and exciting tool to spread the Christian message. Those not comfortable with it must be careful in condemning it. The Bible offers a parallel. Jesus' disciples, filled with the Holy Spirit, picked up teaching and healing people where Jesus left off. The Jewish leaders, thinking they had put an end to that sort of business by crucifying Jesus, called a special meeting to decide what to do with his troublesome followers. The council was all for killing the pesky disciples, too, when one of their wiser members took the floor. Gamaliel reminded the council of a few similar cases and then said, "Keep away from these men and let them alone; for if this plan or this undertaking is of men, it will fail; but if it is of God, you will not be able to overthrow them. You might even be found opposing God!" (Acts 5:38-39).

8
RHYTHM MEETS RELIGION

Rock, AS WE SAW IN chapter three, did not come exclusively from Africa but developed out of many cultural influences in America. Black America's role in forming new kinds of music has been well documented by others. When the lines are drawn, they suggest an interesting conclusion: rock originated out of Christian music.

Richard Stanislaw, *Eternity* magazine music columnist and professor of music at Bloomsburg State College, backs up this assertion. "Rock," he says, "has a special claim to the attention of believers because of its history. Rock was first Christian music, then appropriated by the popular secular culture. Decades before Top 40 radio stations discovered rhythm and blues, the style was almost exclusively used for 'gospel.' "[1]

Many Christians cannot accept the idea of taking rock back to its original purpose. They cannot see how any kind of music with such powerful rhythms, which exerts such a force on our physical senses, can be used for God.

The Devil Made Me Do It!

Problem: Rock is basically a "body" music appealing to people on a sensual level. The driving sound and rhythm seduces the listeners, urging them to indulge in physical pleasures. How can such music communicate anything spiritual?

Those who object to rock's physical side, calling it body music, are most likely referring to rock's simplicity. Rock is a simple, straightforward style of music; listeners can easily apprehend the beat and follow along, tap their feet or clap their hands if they want to. A march can have a similar effect. That's great! People *should* feel free to participate physically when they are moved. (Many Americans have lost the ability to move spontaneously in time to music; their inhibitions have stultified their innate capacity.) Notice that the music does not *make* people clap their hands; many just find it easier to do so with the music than without.

Other kinds of music are more intellectual in their approach. Much of classical music might be called head music since it is more complex and intellectual in nature. However, it has never been satisfactorily explained to me why head music is better or more spiritual than body music. Is rock music wrong because it is easy to feel? Is there something sinful about physical feelings?

My theology tells me that God is interested in all of me —the physical, emotional, mental and spiritual person that I am. I may meet God mind to mind, as many people seem to think is best. More often I meet him when I am

102

working (physical), or in the midst of an enjoyable or even anxious experience (emotional). Or I meet him when I least expect it, when something moves within and my spirit tells me he is near (spiritual). In other words, my relationship with God involves my total self. Why, then, should just one kind of music be considered more appropriate for relating to God than another?

Straight from the Heart

In the Middle Ages, various groups of people "denied the flesh" for God. They starved themselves, dressed in rags, refused to bathe or comb their hair, and when that was not enough, flogged themselves senseless with whips. The idea was that all this "denying" made them more spiritual since they were no longer given over to the gross desires of the body. However, their asceticism did not necessarily make them more spiritual. But it did make them hungry, dirty, smelly, ragged and sore.

While the idea of whipping the body to prove spirituality is not commonly practiced now, people still buy the idea that the body is somehow inferior and should be put in its place to increase spirituality. The body is seen as a stumbling block on the road to heaven. In certain instances, perhaps it is; but it is also our only vehicle for carrying out God's will. God created the whole body; that makes it wholly good, not the seat of sin unimaginable. Every action or desire of the body, after all, originates in the heart.

The accusation that rock music or its beat arouses erotic feelings is weak. The human sexual response is not hormonal, triggered by the presence of hormones in the bloodstream, as in animals (like dogs which go into heat). Although hormones do play a part, the sexual response in human beings is primarily based on experience. It is a *learned* response. Rock's pulsating beat does not interfere

103

with normal internal body chemistry, overstimulating hormones and bringing about sexual excitation. If people get sexually excited merely listening to rock, it is because they have learned to do so. Since it is a learned response, it can be consciously controlled, as can any other aspect of behavior, given sufficient motivation.

Obviously, a man might get excited watching a shapely female wriggle around to a rock beat. I would maintain, however, that this has less to do with the style of music being played than with the visual drama displayed.

Having sexual feelings is not sinful. And acting on sexual feelings is not wrong, provided it is within the framework prescribed by the Bible. What is sinful is indulging in anything (not just sex) at the wrong time, in the wrong quantity or under the wrong circumstances.

Eating, for example, is a very physical activity. We even hold church suppers so we can indulge in this sensual experience with our Christian friends. Yet this simple and basic pleasure can be perverted. Say you have just eaten a fine meal, but suddenly leap from the table, jump into your car and head for the nearest McDonald's to order a Big Mac, large fries and vanilla shake. You do not need the food; you merely like the way it tastes. So you devour more and then still more. Such behavior would be clearly wrong; it would be gluttony. But the Big Mac did not cause the sin.

I believe the apostle Paul spoke to this problem when he said, "To the pure all things are pure" (Tit 1:15). Notice he did not say, "To the pure some things are pure" or "most things are pure." He said *all* things, extending the boundaries quite far indeed.

Christian young people have confided in me guiltily that they "really like rock music"—as if it is something to be ashamed of. They have been made to feel that liking

104

rock indicates a serious moral or spiritual flaw in their character. But Paul's comment at least opens the door for a more liberated approach. For if our attitudes and intentions are pure, how can the object of our desire be otherwise? Furthermore, those fleshly desires we worry so much about would not be a problem if our hearts were right because a right heart moderates all of the body's actions. We have nothing to fear (sex, food, games, drink, music) if our hearts are pure.

Chuck Girard, one of the pioneers of contemporary Christian music, feels rock can be played and enjoyed in a pure way. In an interview, I asked him about this idea.

"An audience can sense where a musician is coming from. If a rock musician gets up and boogies, egoing out on the stage, an audience can sense it. But if he's up there praising God with his talent, then that spirit comes across in his music and validates it. Love Song [one of the first Christian rock bands] is an example of this. I've had people tell me that there was a certain spirit and attitude in the playing of the group that glorified God no matter what we were playing.

"For a Christian musician, it takes a measure of maturity to use rock music with responsibility. But when it's used with the right attitude, the sensual nature of rock is vastly diminished—it becomes a spiritual music."

Naturally, the same could be said for any other kind of music, since what we are dealing with here is the very nature of music itself.

They're Playing My Song
Music can be thought of as pure communication, since in many ways it seems to by-pass the intellect and speak directly to the inner person. This communication is of such a special quality that for thousands of years people have

105

considered music as somewhat mystical or even supernatural. Music is not supernatural, but it is certainly mysterious in the way it involves us.

Music is primarily nonverbal communication—pure expression without words. Even when accompanied by a meaningful lyric, it is the wordless side of music which gives it special effect. If the same meanings and emotions could be as easily expressed in words, there probably would be no need for music. Music is able to impart special meaning to a smile, a longing, the touch of a friend, a kiss. The best verbal attempts often fall miles short of the mark.

The old saw "music is the universal language" is only half true. Music may be universal, but it is a language only to those who can speak its dialect. Just as each separate people creates its own unique modes of expression (style of dress, language, customs), so it cultivates its own musical forms. Music takes on the peculiar ability to communicate to the culture which produces it; outsiders will likely be baffled and confused. This much can be readily observed: the music of one culture will often be totally meaningless to the members of another culture. For example, the music of certain mountain tribes in China seems eerie and otherworldly, to Western ears unintelligible. Yet, it carries unspoken significance to those who understand it.

Music as nonverbal communication, creates a sense of belonging for those who understand it. It is a primary function of music to provide this feeling of belonging. Rock music is extremely effective in speaking to its particular group—young people. It provides them with a feeling of belonging.

All music reaches us this way. Rock is not unique in the way it communicates nonverbally to us. But add to this

106

phenomenon the rapidly degenerating subject matter dealt with in the lyrics of most rock, and a distinctly ugly and malicious animal emerges. An animal capable of devouring or at least maiming or scarring its keepers. Here is where the intent of the music comes into play.

The intent of a song has to do with the type of message the songwriter put into the song, in the words as well as the notes on the paper. The songwriter's intention may be easy to ascertain by looking at the words, but it may not be at all evident what he had in mind. However, when a well-done song is played, there is usually no mistake what the songwriter was communicating. Even when the intent is not easily expressed verbally, the emotional impact of the song is usually unmistakable. In other words, the message comes through loud and clear emotionally, whether or not it is grasped cognitively.

Every churchgoer has had an experience with music's ability to telegraph meaning directly to the heart. As the typical Sunday morning service begins, worshipers file in and take their seats while an instrumental organ prelude calms and quiets, creating a peaceful atmosphere, filling the hearts of the congregation with soothing, worshipful feelings. At the end of the service, the reverberating, forceful chords dismiss the worshipers, challenging them to a week of renewed strength and faith. No one misses the message although no words were sung. It is communicated emotionally.

When the rhythms of rock are put to use with the intention of worship, praise, edification or any other higher purpose, it becomes a distinctly different animal than the raging, devouring beast roaming at large through most rock albums. It is different because it is infused with a different purpose. The higher purpose of Christian rock (if the term can be used) is usually quite clearly telegraphed

107

to the heart of every listener. Stripped of its drugs and booze disposition, its overt sexual connotations, its pandering exploitation, and recharged with positive energy, Christian rock stands far apart from the secular variety. This much can be demonstrated.

Look at the audience of the typical Christian concert: well-behaved, attentive, appreciative, considerate, even though the style of music may be virtually the same as that which stirs up the masses at a Rolling Stones' concert. Quite clearly, people respond to the intent of the music, and to all the attendant stimuli, not the mere rhythm or beat as is so often supposed.

The Devil's Due

Still, rock is viewed as having a rhythm that is intrinsically evil, a thing spawned by the devil to entrap unwary humans, to seduce them and lead them to ruin. Many conscientious religious leaders take this view, adding that anything which the devil has devised cannot contain any spiritual potential. The very form corrupts what it touches; therefore, any enterprise which attempts to use it is doomed from the beginning.

Those who promote such a view are making two serious mistakes simultaneously: overestimating the devil's power and underestimating his subtlety.

Satan is not all-powerful; he does not possess the power to create anything. He can only use whatever we give him, but in that he is virtually unlimited. There seems no end to what he can get from people to use against them. He is well schooled in the weaknesses of the human frame; he knows what we are, and where we are most vulnerable. And he will meet us there, at the point of our greatest weakness.

If one is prone to ego trips, Satan is there. If sex is the

Alice Cooper

Alice Cooper

weak point, he will use that. If money is where the heart is, or power or fame or ambition, Satan will employ that to destroy the soul. If a young person is easily led by the crowd, Satan knows it, and he will use it for his own ends if allowed. He can even use religion. One of his favorite ruses is to allow the security of empty ritual and blind, misguided emotionalism (which distorts true faith and even kills it) to replace spirituality. Thus the victims never perceive their demise, so secure are they in the knowledge that they are very religious and, therefore, safe.

The devil does not care what he uses to undermine the truth. We flatter him in thinking that he creates a special trap or holds sway in a province of his own design. Those who treat rock music as the devil's domain have forgotten that Satan is the father of lies, and chaos is his calling. He can create nothing, only pervert the good things God has created, bending them to his own ends. An error is made, too, in thinking that anything which the devil uses cannot be redeemed.

Music is the work of the all-powerful, eternally loving God who continually redeems his creation. Nothing is beyond his restoring power or ever far from his grace. Thus music, in whatever form, is God's. It therefore need not have a direct spiritual emphasis to be spiritual or to speak to us in a meaningful way. To call something which God has made "satanic" at once magnifies Satan's limited power and diminishes God's supreme authority. That, simply, is blasphemy.

9

A SHEEP
IN
WOLVES' CLOTHING

I HAVE SEEN STRANGE THINGS in church: karate demonstrations, magic shows, chalk talks, singing saws, trained birds, puppets, ventriloquists and more. I have read of preachers practicing all sorts of weirdness to catch the attention of their congregations. The undisputed champion is the minister who doused himself with lighter fluid and set fire to his clothing as he stood in his pulpit, demonstrating to his horrified congregation in a graphic way what he figured the flames of hell would be like. News wires have also carried the story of a converted stripper who now does her "striptease for God," hoping to lure in the unwary with her skills and then shock them with the gospel.

The point of all this craziness is, of course, to attract

attention, draw a crowd. Once you have the curious on-lookers hooked on the show, you can slip in a little good news. That is the idea.

To many, the approach lacks finesse; it smacks of the con game. Show biz and Christianity are not supposed to mix; when they do it causes difficulties. It is like bringing a wolf to town. When everyone gathers around to see the real, live wolf, you suddenly whisk off the pelt and present them with a sheep. That is the problem as many see it.

Sacred Cows and Trojan Horses

Problem: Rock is a Trojan horse trotted out to trick nonbelievers into accepting Christ by giving them what they want rather than what they need. The gospel is compromised and cheapened by such deception and by contact with such a low form of music.

Boiled down, the problem is one of communication; how far are Christians allowed to go in reaching unbelievers? Throughout history Christians have pounced on every new advance in the field of communication to spread the good news. When Johann Gutenberg came up with his notion for moveable type, it was for printing the Bible, not one of his mother's favorite hasenpfeffer recipes. Religious pamphlets, magazines and books of all kinds have poured off the presses ever since. With the advent of radio and television, the public airways were soon abuzz with scores of radio and television evangelists. The PTL Club and Billy Graham's crusades are bounced off satellites to the far corners of the earth. Technology has never remained far beyond the grasp of the church.

Oddly, the Christian art of communication has not kept pace with the hardware. Too often we have used brand new methods to preach an outmoded style. So, for all our space-age gear, we end up talking only to other Chris-

tians. Paul Johnson, a contemporary Christian musician
and composer, puts it well.

*Today the church faces a world that is not the least bit
interested in hearing us defend our sacred cows. It is
interested, however, in hearing the solution to the crises it
faces in the realm of personal identity, economy, ecology,
ethics, guilt, hope for the world's future . . . all of which
have profound solutions in the person of Jesus Christ.*

*As a Christian musician, I find these crises and solu-
tions worthy of musical composition. Indeed, I have discovered that music is one of the most profound methods
of communicating what I believe on these issues. I do
find, however, that the limitations and restrictions
which Christians have placed on sacred music in the
past make my task as a Christian musician in today's
world difficult.*

*If I must limit my method of communication to robed
choirs and a pipe organ to retain a sacred label for my
work as a communicator of the gospel, then my job is de-
feated before it begins.*[1]

Johnson is not the only contemporary musician who has
felt the frustration of trying to fit the everlasting message
to an updated style within the church's narrowly drawn
limits of acceptability. It is not merely a problem of keeping up with the times; there is a basic misunderstanding
of how rock music communicates.

To many traditionalists, the message of rock is drowned
out in the din of screaming guitars and the crashing
rhythms of the drums. They feel that rock, as a low form
of music, is not fit to clothe the heavenly gospel. Thus anything communicated by the flashy style will be cheapened
in the process.

Rock musicians, on the other hand, feel that, to those
familiar with the language of rock, it has a power to speak

where other means fail. There is nothing cheap about that. They see rock as a legitimate way to meet non-Christians on their own territory, to earn the right to be heard by speaking their language.

With a sense of history, one recognizes that this is not an original scheme, but one that has been continually used in the church through the ages.

Give Me That Old Time Religion!

Composers of church music in all eras have struggled to outfit their faith with suitable new music. For the most part it has been a struggle against sentimentality. Christians by and large have a maddening habit of firmly planting themselves at any point where pleasant feelings have touched their faith. They say, "This is good; let's keep it this way," which is often a mistake. Peter made the same sort of error at the transfiguration.

Jesus had taken his three closest disciples up on the mountain with him to witness firsthand his glory undiminished. Peter was especially impressed and fell on his face, crying, "This is wonderful! Let's make three tents, one for you, one for Moses and one for Elijah." He wanted to preserve the moment forever, forgetting that the life Jesus requires is not static but active, not resting on past pleasures or achievements but moving ahead.

Recently, the music director of my church closed the service with the congregation singing an old favorite, Luther's "A Mighty Fortress"—only an upbeat version, heavily syncopated. The congregation, myself included, gamely struggled through the new arrangement, not once but twice, to get the hang of it. After the service I heard many members comment that the new version was interesting, but they preferred the "original." I agreed. In fact, there was quite a lot of grumbling to that effect until we

114

learned that we had indeed sung the original arrangement. We had sung it the way Luther had written it! Most people were upset because it was simply different from the traditional version we usually sing.

Look in any hymnal at the dates of the songs the church is singing: 1742, 1611, 1535, 1409. The dates reach back and back, through the Middle Ages and into the first few centuries of the early church. Of course, the main bulk of our hymns date from the 1800s, deriving from the great revivals of the last century. And there are even a few from the last several decades, included in an effort to remain current. Mostly, the songs we sing in our churches are songs with a long and glorious past. We "moderns" with our almost unlimited access to the past are worse pack rats than our ancestors. The relatively recent capability of instantaneous global communication, and the distribution of knowledge and scholarship that it generates, allows us to hoard, not only the work of the masters, but the work of the not-so-great as well. Our churches end up revering as sacred and everlasting music which was only meant to have a brief life, music which was to speak to a particular time, then give way to something else.

M. Goldbeck, noted music historian, made the observation that until the end of the nineteenth century, music gravitated around the present. The music of the day was always *contemporary*. People in church heard Bach's latest composition as well as a few old favorites.[2] Today, art music orbits the past, around the whole history and tradition of music.

In this, modern Christians have artificially tricked themselves into thinking that contemporary sounds are somehow less worthy of carrying Christian ideals. Yet such a notion never occurred to churchgoers of even two hundred years ago.

115

Martin Luther wrote songs for his reformation effort, giving music back to the common people. Charles Wesley did the same, using drinking songs and fitting them with meaningful Christian messages. Others followed the lead of these reformers until the idea of using common forms of communication to speak to Christians and non-Christians alike was an approved and established practice. However, this was lost somewhere along the way, at least in the area of music.

It is time to bring back the idea of taking a normal, commonly recognized vehicle, such as rock, and putting it into Christian service. We often lose sight of the fact that Christians are a minority of the world's peoples; we rub shoulders daily with a distinctly secular society. Thus, when we present our peculiar world view it is likely to be overlooked.

Communication demands more than just staying current, keeping up with the times. It also requires a knowledge of the person or group being addressed. You have to know who you are talking to.

Rock musicians are convinced that traditional music has little effect on a non-Christian world and virtually none on the rock generation. Singing about "bringing in the sheaves" or "marching to Zion" communicates nothing to those who do not know what sheaves are or where in the world Zion might be. In fact, many of our sacred songs do not have much effect, beyond sentimentality, on most Christians either. Even the most familiar hymns of the church are often sung by rote without any real understanding.

Every Sunday millions of Christians unwittingly make statements in hymns that they would be embarrassed or unwilling to make otherwise. "Take my silver and my gold, not a mite would I withhold...." How many church-

116

goers would volunteer to carry out that declaration as the collection plate passed, and that fine old hymn fresh on their lips? Sometimes the hymns themselves defy common-sense understanding, as in: "That with the world, myself, and thee, I, ere I sleep, at peace, may be," or, "Here I raise My Ebenezer." What *is* my Ebenezer? You must be sharp indeed to unravel the meaning of these phrases, or the host of others like them, which populate church hymnals. Yet who gives them a second thought?

In *Protestant Worship Music,* Charles Etherington makes the observation that part of the unreality which traditional church music has for modern ears lies in the fact that so much of it reflects thoughts and feelings of the past.

Certainly the music cannot mean very much if it is a medium through which people express thoughts that have no meaning for them. . . . Although contemporary music is often considered merely for entertainment value, a person will often come closer to a realization of God's presence through hearing serious music at home or in the concert hall than he does in church. This statement may seem incredible and even shocking to people who are not musically sensitive, but a moment's reflection should persuade them that there is nothing strange in the thought of God making himself felt through any medium that will awaken a response.[3]

Watch Your Language!
The charge that rock is a Trojan horse used to trick nonbelievers into becoming Christians is based on a narrow notion of what evangelism means.

The story is told of a Christian who is out on the street witnessing. Along comes a nonbeliever who inadvertently wanders into range.

117

"Have you heard the good news?"

"No, what is it?" the nonbeliever asks enthusiastically.

"You're going to hell!" the Christian bellows righteously.

The bewildered non-Christian scratches his head, plucks up his courage and asks, "What's the *bad* news?"

Regrettably, this little scenario is less fictitious than many Christians would care to admit. We frequently make one of two mistakes when we set out to talk to non-Christians. Either we speak to other Christians and hope non-Christians are listening somewhere close by and somehow get the message, or we plunge headlong into an invasion of non-Christian territory, guns blazing, expecting a fight. Both mistakes are ill-fated, because they make non-Christians run for cover.

Have you ever watched television on Sunday morning? The airwaves are sewed up by big-name evangelists who beam their church services from their modern multi-million-dollar temples. The evangelists preach sincere messages which implore nonbelievers to let Christ into their lives so they can be as happy as we all can see that they, the evangelists, are. The shows are generally well produced, run like clockwork and usually include an invitation for non-Christians to respond.

But who is watching those shows? Other Christians, overwhelmingly. The typical supporter for these shows is a white southern female aged forty-five to sixty. We hope that by chance some non-Christians might stumble over the program as they spin their channel selector. And, of course, some do.

Have you ever tuned in to a religious radio station? What you usually hear is a thunder-throated preacher booming out the salvation plan for one and all, telling non-Christians how evil, mean, wicked, bad and nasty they really are. He tells them they are lost in sin, doomed to everlasting fire, and worse. Then he tells them how to get right with God. God does not want to send anyone to hell, but he will. Oh, yes, he will.

If you had a message to give to some Chinese, would you insist that they first learn English before you deliver the message? No, you would find a way to translate your message so they could understand it.

To non-Christians, Christianity is a foreign language they do not comprehend. Yet, we think if we just keep talking at them, they will somehow learn the language. So we preach and preach and preach. Our actions preach, our music preaches—all in our peculiar language. Rarely does anyone try to learn the non-Christian's language before starting in on the preaching. But the basic principle of evangelism should be communication, and communicating the good news involves identifying with people, speaking their language.

Rock communicates to the rock crowd. It has the ability to reach a population that has grown up with it. Young people identify with it readily, much more so than with, for example, the elaborate Sunday morning television pageants which give Christians a good feeling but often do little for non-Christians.

Rock music is music in the language of the rock generation. Our message can be carried effectively through it. Those who say that this somehow compromises the gospel are forgetting one thing: communication *is* compromise. You talk; I listen. And vice versa. Without this basic agreement, nothing happens. In true communication both parties must be free and open to the needs of the other; speakers must speak to listeners in ways they can understand; otherwise, speech is meaningless.

Just because I speak in a way you can understand does

not mean that I have compromised my message, only the way I say it.

Blind Fools and Other Aberrations
Some influential religious leaders have utterly damned rock, feeling that since its language is beyond comprehension (to them), it cannot communicate to anyone else. People like evangelist Jimmy Swaggart, have spoken out on this point, becoming standard bearers in the crusade against rock in general and Christian rock in particular.

Jimmy Swaggart no doubt spoke for many when he said, "Contemporary [Christian rock] has become the order of the day on most of your Christian radio stations. Yet, the words have little if any meaning, the lyrics seem to say nothing." He continues, "The chord structure of contemporary music seems to meander off in every possible direction, with no mode nor method. The message (if it had one) is lost within the odd and strange sounds that would pass for a melody."

Swaggart continues, "I emphatically state that it's *impossible* to touch anyone's heart with contemporary music. It's impossible because the meaning is disjointed. It may be desired by certain elements in the body of Christ because it sounds so much like the world, but it does not elicit a response from their heart toward God."[4]

Swaggart's comments reveal more about himself than about his intended subject. Anyone who has listened to a rock record album or attended a rock concert could tell him this music communicates. Anyone who has listened to or read the lyrics of contemporary Christian songs knows that the message comes through loud and clear. Jimmy Swaggart has not been listening.

There are others who believe as Swaggart does, and there would be no need to single him out if he had kept his views to himself. Unfortunately, Jimmy Swaggart is a nationally recognized evangelist who has singled himself out on the topic. The above comments were made in his magazine, *The Evangelist,* which is reported to have a circulation in excess of 450,000 readers. Thus, his uninformed views are spread far and wide across the nation.

Bob Larson, another itinerant evangelist, picked up the antirock banner in the early seventies and wrote two books, *Rock and the Church* and *The Day Music Died.* While more reasoned in their approach than Swaggart, both books set the tone for the fight against rock music for the years to come.

More recently, Larson has added another book to his credits. This one, entitled simply *Rock,* appears to back away from some of the more strident excesses of his previous works. He allows that maybe Christian rock is all right after all as an alternative to the bad rock music of the secular world. However, in the final analysis, this book does not move much beyond his previous positions, though inflamatory style has given way to a more moderate approach.

These men and others like them, who set themselves up as authorities, as experts in the eyes of many trusting souls, do great violence to the work of countless numbers of their brothers and sisters who are actively trying to do God's will, using rock to speak to a dying world. In the end they do violence to God's work, too. Their views are passed around, augmented and used like whips to herd people into corrals of conformity. Of course, this drives away as many as it herds together.

Jesus encountered such activity frequently in his lifetime. His term for people who attempted to straitjacket their brothers in the name of spirituality was "blind fools."

121

Mr. Booth's Brass Band

Actually, Christian rock musicians seek to do only what William Booth, founder of the Salvation Army, did with his brass bands toward the end of the last century. Brass bands, you must understand, did not meet with the full approval of the religious-minded of that day. Booth's small touring groups were subject to heckling and embarrassment. Their meetings were broken up on occasion by drivers herding horses and buggies through the scattering streetside throng. But the idea survived to become an institution of its own within the Salvation Army.

On Christmas of 1879 Booth wrote, "Every note, and every strain, and every harmony is divine and belongs to us." And he ordered Christians to "bring out your cornets and harps and organs and flutes and violins and pianos and drums, and everything else that can make a melody. Offer them to God, and use them to make all the hearts about you merry before the Lord."[5]

To the average person on the street today, the words "Salvation Army Band" conjure up a quaint image of a bygone era. But the idea behind it is still a good one: take the message to the people who need to hear it in a form they can understand and respond to.

I am not suggesting that we do away with everything that has gone before, only that we should make room for Christian rock artists to take their place among all the others who have given meaningful expression to our faith. For there are many among us who desperately seek what we all need: a music which expresses rather than alienates itself from our deepest convictions, which does not pander to us but enobles us by its self-conscious dedication to the glory of God.

122

10

YOU GOTTA' HAVE ART

EVER SEE ANYBODY TRY TO row a boat with one oar? Or see a sailboat traverse a lake without a rudder? It can't be done. No sailor would willingly put to sea in a ship without oars or a rudder. To do so would be foolish, possibly disastrous.

Yet, every day, thousands of people put to sea in ships that have neither oars nor rudder—nor compass. They are young people who come of an age to begin thinking for themselves, but have not been given the proper equipment for making the right decisions, for steering themselves through life.

A good example of this is my friend Gary. Gary grew up in a family that did not believe in going to movies. Sometimes there would be a movie which my parents would allow me to see, and I would invite Gary. But the answer was always the same: no movies. Later, as we grew older and entered high school, Gary was left to make those kinds of decisions on his own. Consequently, he started going to every movie that came to town. It did not matter what it was; Gary would watch it. The best movies and the absolute worst alike, Gary watched them all.

I went with him to a double feature once. After the first movie I asked him, "How did you like it?"

"Great," he said. When the second show was over he said, "Man, that was great, too."

"What are you talking about?" I asked, shocked. "That was an *awful* movie. A disaster!"

A funny look came over him. "Oh" was all he said. He could not tell the difference; all he knew was that he liked movies. As elementary as it seems, no one had ever told him how to tell the good ones from the bad ones, how to choose which ones to watch and which to stay away from. To him they were all the same.

Those who condemn all of rock have created thousands of Garys, people who cannot tell good music from bad because they have never been given guidelines for judging it.

In this way, those violently opposed to rock have done a great disservice to young people. Because of their total condemnation ("Rock is wrong; don't listen to any of it") they have left thousands of people with no way to effectively judge a large part of contemporary culture. And without guidelines, it is only too easy to drift into confusion and error. Sooner or later people must be allowed to think and choose for themselves how they will live. It would be far better to provide a good foundation and training in making the right decisions before that time comes.

A good foundation consists of knowing what is good and

124

Chuck Barry

what is bad, and the ability to tell them apart. When you know what is good and how to recognize it, the choice is easy. However, when it comes to art (and when we talk about music we are talking about art), most people do not know what makes good art good, or how to recognize it.

Admittedly, this is not an easy thing to do, especially without training. Art does not come affixed with a pre-pasted label which neatly lumps it into one of two categories: classic or garbage. Everything of artistic endeavor exists on a continuum, a wide spectrum which spans the gulf between that which could be considered superior or good, and that which is inferior or bad.

Music, like painting, theater, literature, sculpture, pottery, dance and all the rest of art, must exhibit that vital spark which allows it to transcend the mere mechanics of its creation if it is to be judged superior. Good music, in whatever style, must possess all the qualities we have come to expect of good art: uniqueness, craftsmanship, maturity, intelligence, wholeness and spontaneity.

Clearly, an entire style of music cannot be good or bad; only individual pieces of music can be labeled. The better we understand the qualities of the good, the better able we will be to tell the good from the bad in rock music (or any other kind of music or art for that matter). Here are some qualities of good art.

Uniqueness: This is the attribute of originality, of never having been before. A work bearing this trait will seem new and novel, and to a certain extent, inventive. It says, "I am one of a kind."

Craftsmanship: This refers to the technical aspect of the work, how well it is made. Whether referring to a sculpture or a song, the skill of the maker will be apparent. Good art reflects a high degree of skill. Also, the skill must be inherent to the medium. For example, a sculp-

126

tor and a potter may both work in clay, but they will do very different things with it. Their skills are not the same. You cannot say to the potter, "You are a poor craftsman because you can't make a lifelike statue," or say to the sculptor, "You lack the proper skills because your work is not functional." Those statements are nonsense because potters and sculptors are working in different mediums, even if they are working with the same materials. It is the same with music. Whether a rock song or a symphony, the work should say, "I was made by an expert."

Maturity: When you think of something being mature, you think of it being fully developed. A work which fails to reach its full potential and remains at an elementary level can be said to be infantile, lacking in maturity. This does not mean there is no place for the simple, the basic, the profound. Often the highest expression of maturity is found in the studied application of the most basic elements. A mature work will say, "I am full-grown."

Intelligence: In order for any piece of art to be considered good, it must be understandable. It must be a work of reason; that is, it must show us something of the mind of its creator. An intelligent work will show a degree of imagination, cleverness and perhaps wit. Rather than presenting a jumble of half-formed ideas, good art shows the work of the mind in selecting, assembling and developing its raw materials. It must reveal intelligence in design and require reason and logic to fully apprehend its beauty. Art with intelligence says, "I am refined."

Wholeness: As with a good story, a good song must satisfy the listener; there can be no loose ends and no missing pieces. Wholeness means that a particular work has made full use of its opportunities and that it stands alone as a finished entity. In a sense, a whole work fulfills our expectations, delivering all it promises. It is not fragmented or

127

made from patches. Its parts have been totally unified. A work with the quality of wholeness says, "I am complete."

Spontaneity: In art, spontaneity does not mean that a work suddenly springs into existence full-blown. However, many works of art appear as if they *were* instantaneously created. They have a lively, animated appearance, capable of engaging their audience. An artist may have slaved for years over a work, pouring out his or her soul upon it, but the piece must never appear forced or stale or workworn. Spontaneity also suggests that the work has a life of its own, apart from the artist. It sometimes appears that the work has always existed. The great Michelangelo once made a comment to the effect that the subjects of his sculptures already lived within the mighty blocks of marble; he only carved away the stone to set them free. A work with spontaneity says, "I am alive."

For most of the rock audience, and even the most discriminating critics, it would be enough to be given good art. But for Christians, that is not enough; we must also be concerned with the music's *message.*

The Four Arts
In his book, *Art and the Bible,* Francis Schaeffer describes four categories of art: bad art with a true message; good art with a true message; bad art with a false message; and good art with a false message.[1] These are what I call the four arts, and they all abound in the soup of the contemporary music scene. Good and bad art with their respective messages exist side by side and back to back in the music world. Listen to any Top-40 radio station; you will hear from fifteen to twenty different songs in an hour, each with a different message.

Christians, desiring truth in all areas of life, require

true messages in music as well. Sorting out true messages from false ones is not hard in itself, but when music is added to give impetus to the message, it tends to confuse things. The distinctions blur; gray areas appear. If the music is catchy and the lyrics pleasing, listeners could find themselves accepting a message they might otherwise reject.

In this regard, one of the four arts is quite treacherous. Bad art with a true message is not likely to make much of an impact; the message, despite its worth, is buried under the inferiority of the music. The same could be said for bad art with a false message. People seldom take bad art seriously; whatever message accompanies it is not taken seriously either.

Good art operates in reverse of that principle. Good art with a true message is held in high esteem; the message is reinforced by the quality of the art. This is the best, but danger lies close by. When good art is coupled with a false message, the message gains importance. It takes on a credibility it would not and could not and should not ordinarily have. In responding to the goodness of the art, people may suspend judgment and accept the false message, too.

I do not mean to suggest, as some do, that rock performers actually *try* to trick people into believing something that is false; it just happens. In the clash between the images and illusions of the rock world, rock singers are likely to say things in public and in song which they do not necessarily believe. What they say is often part of a public image; it usually has no direct bearing on reality. Or else they speak to a commonly assumed reality, such as "love makes the world go round," "you only live once; so grab all you can get," "happiness is all that matters" and the like. These are nothing more than the myths of

129

the modern world. Rock singers do not have to believe these myths to sing songs about them; many performers assume these fanciful sentiments are what their audiences want to hear. Time and again rock musicians come back to certain stock themes for their songs, themes which are almost universally accepted without question.

Generally speaking, when it comes to communicating true messages, rock falls down in the following areas:

Materialism: Although many songwriters point out that wealth and material things can never insure happiness, a good many more say just the opposite. Success is often pictured as obtaining more goods than someone else, getting your share, making your fortune, having fame getting power. Conspicuous consumption is the order of the day. Christians know this philosophy to be false, and the Bible offers plenty of evidence against it.

Sex: Love in rock is usually physical love. Both men and women are seen as sexual objects which exist solely to satisfy the needs of the other. Relationships in songs often focus on the sex act as the ultimate expression of love. This is love, of course, on its most immature and selfish level. The Bible puts a wholly different value on sex; Christians recognize many dimensions of the word *love* rarely portrayed in song. Yet rock is usually content to mirror the immature aspects of sexual love, rather than explore the subject on a more mature level.

Hedonism: The good life is exalted in rock continually. Self-indulgence is looked upon as a personal right. "If it feels good, do it" is the motto. Personal pleasure is the highest aim in life; you are to deny yourself nothing toward attaining your pleasure. The biblical idea that we are to *serve* others is foreign to most popular songs.

There are undoubtedly many other themes which could be identified, but these few suffice for the bulk of popular music. Not all songs have clearly defined themes; their messages may be mixed, containing elements of many different themes. Some songs are subtle in their suggestions; others are blatant, actively presenting views that leap into direct conflict with Christian values. And of course many songs present true messages, even though they are not written or performed in a Christian context. Jackson Browne's "Rock Me on the Water" is such a song. Another example is the song "Love is the Answer," made popular by England Dan and John Ford Coley. The song became a hit, topping the charts on the strength of a plaintive chorus that beseeched the, "Light of the World" to shine on us and set us free to love one another. It held love as the answer to our various human problems. For most listeners these songs and the numerous others like them are gentle expressions of a higher humanity. For others, these songs express a distinctly Christian sentiment.

Use It or Lose It

So, in the tangle of mixed messages presented by popular music, it is left to the listener to decide what is true and what is false in a song, to embrace the truth and reject the lie. That is using good discrimination, being your own critic. I believe all Christians are called to be discriminating listeners, not only of rock music but of everything they hear. If we desire the privilege of listening to rock music, both Christian rock and the music of the larger community, we must seize the responsibility of thinking about what is being listened to and weeding out the good from the bad by applying the standards of good art and by examining the message.

Everyone must become a critic—weighing the difference between what is acceptable and what is unacceptable in rock music—or forfeit the right to choose. There are plenty of people who are eager to dictate what we ought to listen to. There are many self-appointed guardians of the airwaves. In essence, they say, "We don't think people are capable of deciding for themselves what to listen to. So no one should listen to any of it. Throw it all out." Sadly, many Christians, to avoid having to decide for themselves, have abdicated their thinking to others.

I believe it is every Christian's right and responsibility to decide how he or she will relate to the world. This is part of the freedom Christ came to give us. It is a precious freedom and should not be abandoned or abused.

When it comes to music, we should all be aware of what we are listening to and how it is affecting us. For those not used to paying such close attention to what is being heard, it might mean making a conscious effort to discern a song's message as well as its emotional effect. This can be done by simply asking a few questions: What am I feeling? Is this healthy? Is this consistent with my faith? Does the song's message go against any of the basic truths Christians live by? A conscious effort to answer those questions should result in the ability to judge whether or not to continue listening to a particular song or a certain group.

Deciding that a certain song has a true message does not mean merely that we agree with what is being said or that it makes us feel good. A song may have a true message, yet make us uncomfortable. For example, knowing that millions of the world's people are starving daily is not particularly pleasant to think about, and does not make anyone feel good. It is true nonetheless. On the other hand, a Christian song implying that "if you'll only trust Jesus he'll give you everything you want," might cause good feelings, but it offers a false message. A song is not true just because it has the words *Jesus* or *God* in it.

132

Neither is a song false because it omits those words. As I have said before, each song must be weighed carefully to determine the truth of its message. This applies to all music and to all art.

Once a song is found to be unacceptable, must it be completely censored? The answer to that question is maybe. Only the individual listener can determine that, and each must decide for him or herself, depending upon his or her own inner strength. For example, if a song is very persuasive, and you find yourself doubting something you know to be right, then you probably should stop listening to it, acting as your own board of censors and cutting that song out of your program. However, another Christian may find the song unobjectionable; he or she may not be affected in the same way as you are by that same song. You cannot decide that he or she should not listen to it; you can only decide for yourself and explain why you think the song is harmful.

If we wish to be allowed freedom to listen, or not to listen, to the music we choose, then we must allow others to make their own choices, too. And we must honor their decisions. That is the essence of tolerance.

Tolerance is one virtue sadly in short supply in the Christian community. Many have been quick to condemn rock music. Those who forcefully denounce rock have been obliged to condemn Christian rock music along with the rest.

Again, Jimmy Swaggart elucidates the opinion of many when he states, "I maintain that it's impossible to worship God by contemporary music. . . . Contemporary is the surrogate to the acid-rock type music in the world. . . . There is no substance whatever relative to the word of God or worship. It's ludicrous as far as meaning is concerned. The sounds are weird, strange, and odd; correspondent to the minds of the individuals who relate to this type of music. There is very little knowledge of God there or else they would not be bent in this direction. . . . This *stuff* is like the world. It does not bring glory to God."[2]

I know Swaggart is wrong because I have been touched by Christian rock music; it spoke to me at a time in my life when nothing else did. In a real sense it changed my life. For although I was a Christian, there were still areas in my life where I had not allowed God full control. Then one night I heard a Christian rock group playing in a park. I sat down and listened, and a new person went home that night. I was moved toward a deeper relationship with God, and I have always considered that night, and that group with their music, a turning point. They showed me that it was possible to live as a Christian in the modern world without being irrelevant, old-fashioned or hopelessly bound by unthinking dogma.

Since then I have attended many contemporary Christian concerts where I have seen others touched in the same way I was; I have seen them built up through rock music. I have received letters from people whose lives have been healed by God speaking through Christian rock music. I have seen God's hand moving among thousands of people in this way. There are now hundreds of young churches which present contemporary Christian music in their services almost exclusively, and those churches are growing.

How can one find fault with the method God uses to reveal himself? The Pharisees held much the same complaint about Jesus: his ways were just not "religious" enough for them. Jesus warned them that by condemning him they were also condemning God. Blasphemy, Jesus said, is denying the work of God's Spirit. Many have put themselves in that same, dangerous position, denying the

134

active work of God in bringing people to himself through Christian rock music.

The Bible tells the story of a visit Jesus made to the home of his good friends, Mary, Martha and Lazarus (Lk 10:38-42). Jesus was greeted by Martha and welcomed into her home. She scurried around looking after all the preparations for the big meal she had planned. I suppose that as she hurried to get things in order, it suddenly dawned on her that she was working alone—where was Mary? She looked up and there was Mary sitting with Jesus, deep in conversation with him. Martha was immediately angry; she was doing her part, and here was Mary, chatting idly away with so much yet to be done. "Lord, doesn't it seem unfair to you that I have to do all the work while Mary just sits?" she asked. And before Jesus could even respond, she answered the question herself. "Tell her to come and work with me."

Although Mary and Martha were sisters, with a common background, heritage and family life, they were different. Although they both loved Jesus and were loved by him, they expressed that love in different ways, Martha through serving Christ, and Mary in communion with him. And I think Jesus appreciated them both, one just as much as the other. He did not expect them to act the same or to love him in the same way; he knew they were different. He knew there was a place for Martha in the kitchen, and a place for Mary in the parlor. But there was no place for one to sit in judgment over the other. That is why Jesus said, "Martha, dear friend, you are upset over all these details. There is really only one thing worth being concerned about. Mary has discovered it, and I won't take it away from her." Loving him was the important thing, and he was not about to discourage Mary, or make her join her sister in the kitchen.

135

We must allow others to serve Christ and express their love for him in ways that are natural to them, and therefore best for them. It is not fair to expect all believers to express their faith and their love for Christ in the same way. It is equally unfair to judge other Christians because their expressions of love and faith are different from our own. Martha's sin was not so much in worrying over details but in condemning Mary for not doing as she did. Jesus offered her a gentle reprimand and declined to choose sides in the matter. He understood that for faith to be meaningful, people had to be able to honor and worship God freely in their own way.

We must arrive at this same tolerance regarding music. Our musical tastes are our own. No Christian should be belittled for liking rock music; conversely, those who like rock should refrain from condemning music which others find meaningful.

If we are to love as Christ loves, then we must accept those with differing musical tastes and accept their right to listen to the music they find meaningful. Rather than condemning rock, God's people should be in the position of encouraging whatever is good, worthy and true in popular music. Where wrongs have been committed, where error is practiced, we need a vigorous demonstration of the truth. Rather than fettering or shackling our Christian artists, we must encourage them to higher achievement. For the Christian community and the world at large desperately need the creativity, enthusiasm, courage and vision Christian artists can bring.

Appendix:
A Brief History of Rock

Rock music, like many other significant, cultural expressions, can be a useful social indicator. Whenever large numbers of people, the masses, congregate around a central totem, that is cause for study. Rock has become a totem of sorts for the modern age. Divisive for some and unifying for others, rock remains, to many, one cultural institution forever beyond comprehension. Yet rock can be understood as a means of social expressions, for its history—like all history—is the story of people.

Rock was an outlaw straight from the gun. Whatever its origins, either in the Black rhythm and blues of the forties or in the hillbilly honky-tonk of country swing, it first raised its unruly head as rebellion incarnate.

The first certified rocker, Bill Haley (along with his

Comets), did not fit the part exactly. While Haley's music ignited the fans and caused public commotion wherever he went, the group itself was over the hill, more like sedate uncles than outlaws to be emulated. While parents tore at their hair and moaned over their children's lost innocence, the kiddies scanned the horizon for a figure more fitting to wear the newly woven mantle of rock 'n' roll idol.

The mantle fell on Elvis Presley, a Memphis-raised Southern son, and suited him perfectly. He was at once more daring, more dangerous, more unpredictable and thus more exciting than Haley or any five of his Comets. Elvis was made for rock 'n' roll and was in turn made by it. While he personally stood for mother, loyalty, home and apple pie, he was painted large as a rock 'n' roll hooligan, a wayward son, a prodigal with riot in his heart. He reigned supreme and unchallenged in the early years of rock, the midfifties, and the whole era took on his particular image: something dark, menacing, barely under control.

It seemed like Elvis would rule forever, but others were already at work, muscling in on the king's territory. The public outrage at the rebellious rock and the scandals over payola forced the young and growing music industry to police itself. As the fifties headed into their final years, it looked like rock 'n' roll would be its own first casualty.

The rebellious image of the midfifties was replaced by an image of sweetness and light. By 1958 the scene was dominated by all-American, clean-cut, wholesome types suitable for teen consumption. The guys (all Bobbies—Bobby Vinton, Bobby Vee, Bobby Rydell) wore letter sweaters and loafers with neatly pressed pants and well-groomed hair. The girls wore fluffy dresses with matching bows in their bouffant hairdos. Pretty tame.

138

By 1959 real rock 'n' roll had been driven off the air by schmaltzy, syrupy sentimental tripe which was touted as rock, but lacked any real rock bones in its skeleton. As the decade ended, the fans were clamoring for something meaningful in their music, and they found what they were looking for—folk music.

Folk music was a lot of things, but it was primarily *relevant* music. It had a conscience. Folk music had been around forever, waiting in the wings, but now it had center stage with groups like the Weavers starting the folk show rolling. The Kingston Trio, three nice, bright Ivy-Leaguers who sang well and stayed out of trouble, was followed closely by Peter, Paul and Mary who sang even better but did not stay out of trouble. They went places with their music, to marches and rallies and protests. The image was *concern*. Folk music cared. Even people who disliked rock could not knock the new conscientiousness of popular music.

Folk music also had another ace in its hat. It sounded good. It used acoustic instruments instead of electric, and it blended voices melodically. There was nothing disturbing about the sound (although the lyrics were growing more disturbing all the time). The image of concern was admirable and provided a unifying factor for young people which popular music had lacked since the demise of true rock 'n' roll.

Folk music, already linked with protest by Peter, Paul and Mary, was to be firmly entrenched in political involvement with Joan Baez and Bob Dylan. Civil rights became an issue and popular music was there; it had developed a serious side not seen before.

This serious music demanded that people take it seriously. In coffee houses (which had suddenly sprung up to showcase the new folk talents) and campuses, people

139

flocked together to sit quietly and take in the sound in an intellectual atmosphere. The result was that music began to take on awareness. It called people to become socially and politically active. And people responded. This was only one step away from another major image swing: revolution.

Important stage setting had been done by folk music. Whatever else it communicated, it told its listeners that anyone could play music. Thousands were picking up guitars and banjos, learning a few rudimentary chords and adding well-known songs to their repertoire. Soon it would also be demonstrated that anyone could write a song as well. The man responsible for this was Bob Dylan.

Dylan wrote songs like a gambler dealing out cards. At first they were picked up by other folk singers and added to their albums. Then he began singing them on record himself. His voice was hardly attractive—an unbelievable nasal whine. Whereas Peter, Paul and Mary and Joan Baez had pretty, well-polished voices, Dylan's was ragged and grating. But it was real.

By 1963 folk music had captured the mass of the market. The guitar had become an almost universal symbol of protest. (Pete Seeger, a most outspoken member of the Weavers, had his head handed to him by the Hough Committee on Un-American Activities for his "leftist" political leanings.) The land was stirring and folk music turned bitter.

Bob Dylan was at the front of the growing movement. Jahn notes that "Dylan was the first young singer to laud his political awareness in song, and before long his name became synonymous with youth revolt."[1] The music was quickly turning militant. And why not? The world was militant. Race riots, Cuban missiles, bomb shelters, boycotts and other atrocities made it clear that the world was

140

no bed of petunias. Popular music had gone from rock 'n' roll with its image of individual rebellion to folk with its image of social revolution. The very thing that many had hoped would deliver the masses from the grip of "that monstrous noise" had turned into quite a different monster itself. Many people were left wondering, "Whatever happened to that good ol' rock 'n' roll?"

A great many changes had happened in a few quick years. The record business had gone from an emphasis on 45s or singles to albums. Radios and record players were now standard teen commodities. The limited appeal of rock 'n' roll had been broadened and deepened by folk music. Lyrics to pop songs were now regarded as serious music literature. Young people regarded themselves as responsible members of society and were unified to an extent that they had never been before.

As the world entered the midsixties it seemed to hold its breath. Tremors underfoot indicated an earthquake of considerable force was building up. The source of these tremors was the little kingdom in the middle of the sea —Great Britain.

The Beatles, already having conquered their homeland, rolled across America in a flash flood of enthusiasm and acceptance. The sound was contagious, refreshingly young and crazy. People who had spent the last few years being deadly serious now found time to be young again and found that they liked it.

Beatlemania was at first considered to be merely another harmless teen preoccupation, like hula-hoops and Davey Crockett caps. The four mop-tops were charming, fairly well-mannered and delightfully witty. In a word, they were intelligent. And their music was also somewhat intelligent.

The sound of Beatle music was called rock. It was like

rock 'n' roll, but it wasn't rock 'n' roll exactly. It was distinctly different. It was rock 'n' roll filtered through a different culture and remixed. In the process the music lost several ingredients (earthiness, suggestiveness, dependence on the beat) and it gained much more (a wider spectrum of expression, fresh interpretation, complexity).

In 1964 popular music could be summed up in one word: Beatles. They had created a sound which knocked the pop generation on its ear, and everybody was listening.

We were driving through Colorado and we had the radio on and eight of the Top Ten songs were Beatles songs. In Colorado! 'I Want to Hold Your Hand,' all those early ones.

They were doing things nobody was doing. Their chords were outrageous, just outrageous, and their harmonies made it all valid. . . . But I kept it to myself that I really dug them. Everybody else thought they were for the teenyboppers, that they were gonna pass right away. But it was obvious to me that they had staying power. I knew they were pointing the direction where music had to go . . . in my head, the Beatles were it. In Colorado, I started thinking but it was so far out I couldn't deal with it–eight in the top ten.

It seemed to me a definite line was being drawn. This was something that had never happened before.

Bob Dylan, 1971[2]

It wasn't long before Bob Dylan traded his acoustic guitar for one with volume controls, and plugged in himself. World events continued to heat up, but 1964 remained a daffy respite from the grim realities shaping up around the globe.

The following year, 1965, was different right out of the gate. America was awash in two-bit British groups of little consequence. The real forces of music were newly formed American groups which had climbed on the rock bandwagon with the Beatles but didn't even try to imitate them. They guessed, and rightly so, that rock had a rubber soul which could be stretched to infinity. There was no need for imitation.

The Beatles continued to carve a mighty swath, but other groups—the Byrds, Dylan backed by his own rock band (for this he was labeled a folk traitor), and Simon and Garfunkel—quickly surfaced in their wake. Folk music had shown that popular music could be serious and intelligent, and the Beatles had shown that rock with its explosive vitality could be intelligent and literate too. The marriage of rock to the seriousness of folk was perfect. The new groups reveled in this union and the honeymoon began.

Protest songs were a dead end by 1965. The idealism of the folk singers had been replaced by a growing sense of helplessness. Young people had felt that they *could* make a difference, but were disillusioned because things had only gotten worse. All the marches and rallies had done no good. Besides, the evidence of the Kennedy assassination and the looming specter of the Vietnam War defied rational belief. "The world is in chaos," the singers said. "What good does protest do? And anyway, what do you protest against? *Everything* is messed up!" This feeling was given force by the restless energy of rock, and suddenly music was more than just something to listen to. It, like folk music in a more limited way, was socially significant.

Once plugged into this new source, Dylan proved himself to be a dynamo. His personal accomplishments, the near-perfect fusion of words and music, were equaled only by the tremendous influence he wielded over the whole host of other musicians. He was the musician's musician. The Beatles may have been vastly more popular, and wrote arguably superior melodies, but Dylan's influence reached even them.

Other things were happening in popular music in 1965. The record charts for that single year indicate more diversity in style and execution than at any other time. There was still some folk and lots of folk rock; soul music climbed into a place of prominence providing the romantic relief; the Rolling Stones got rolling, proving that rock had a hard, angry side; country western music flirted with the charts.

The pop music throne which had been ruled by Britain was picked up and moved bodily to California. The Beatles still reigned but began taking their cues from the west coast.

Although nobody seemed to notice at the time, 1966 was a year of major transition. The freshness of rock evaporated in a rush of commercialism. Record companies signed up everyone who could play a guitar or drum, flooding the market with cheap imitations of the best groups. The record-buying public turned restlessly from one group to another, trying to satisfy a growing hunger for quickly diminishing uniqueness. The same thing had happened to rock 'n' roll circa 1958 when Elvis had faltered.

As the year closed, strange rumblings were being heard underground, rumblings which, when it was later analyzed, everyone would point to and say, "Yes, it was there all along." Hippydom was sprouting like a mushroom; the "Underground Society" was beginning to bloom.

By the spring of 1968 San Francisco was the capital of the music kingdom. "If you're going to San Francisco, be sure to wear some flowers in your hair . . ." were lyrics to a song many people took literally, piling into minibuses and vans and heading to Love City. Drugs began taking on importance in a self-conscious way. Young people were

144

now thinking of themselves as a single entity, a race. Drugs, free love, long hair were badges you wore to identify yourself as part of the family. (Many parts of the country were "backward" in this regard; some geographical areas refused to allow drugs, free sex or long hair, but young people still identified with the movement and participated wherever and whenever they could.)

Drugs were an ideal ticket into the hippie culture. First they were forbidden—excellent for creating instant desirability and cohesiveness among those who want to be thought of as outside the normal flow. Second, drugs gave young people a separate society with its own language, folk wisdom and rituals. Not that many really liked drugs, and drugs would probably have been replaced by something else if the constant persecution by the straight society had not hardened the resolve to overcome.

The music that emerged from this milieu was a sort of candy: brittle on the outside yet soft-centered. It talked mostly of tuning in, dropping out and breaking free. Different groups formed to emphasize these notions in different ways. Jimi Hendrix, the Doors, Buffalo Springfield and Jefferson Airplane most notably laid down the soundtrack for many minds. At the same time a fortress mentality was developing, reinforced through music, as friction between youth culture and the rest of society began to heat things up.

The Summer of Love would probably have ended quaintly and quietly if not for a major shot in the arm by a group which had been strangely quiet for a long period of time. That group was the Beatles, once again. They had quit touring altogether and let it be known that they were working miracles in the secret confines of their studio. *Sgt. Pepper's Lonely Heart's Club Band* came out of the studio on the run and raced straight to the top. It

145

became the anthem of the hip culture. It was plastic, fantastic and utterly incredible, starting waves of innovation in recording and production that still ripple through the industry today.

The music of the period was just that, music tied to a specific time and place. Most critics of popular music agree that the music produced in that heady time now sounds painfully outdated; removed from context it shrivels like a hothouse plant.

But the music was also drawing attention from the rest of society, not all of it favorable. Rock had taken on a threatening edge; those outside the hip culture were afraid of it. William Shafer, in *Rock Music,* makes this observation: "Expressions surfacing in rock were not always pleasant; they invaded censored or suppressed areas of thought, probing not just sex and sensuality but the pornography of power, the morass of conventional politics, hypocrisies, and inhibitions of our society. The pulpit, press and PTA howled; middle-aged sensibilities were wounded by the frankness of this music."[3]

The war which now broke over rock made 1956's rock 'n' roll seem like a tornado in a teacup. The same arguments were dragged out and pressed into service, but most dyed-in-the-T-shirt radicals were too far gone to respond or care. Those who bore the brunt of the attack were middle-class kids who lived at home and struggled to emulate the freedom of others they saw around them. Growing long hair and wearing funny clothes became outrageous social issues.

The social revolution, which had been hinted at in folk music and nurtured in early rock, boiled over its small psychedelic container and flowed out onto the land. The year 1968 saw music become a nail-splitting monster, forged with hammer and tongs in the fire of controversy.

146

Vietnam had developed into a full-scale war and an embarrassment to the country attending it. To politically-aware young people it was further proof that adult society was out to destroy the world or kill as much of it as they could before handing it over. The activists wanted the world in one piece, and they wanted it *now!* Music reflected this anger, hopelessness and urgency. The picture which developed was not suitable for framing.

Popular music did a chameleon trick in 1968; psychedelia was itself a chameleon, changing constantly, taking on whatever color it was thrown up against. It was hard when it wanted to protest, soft when it wanted to love, snappy and singable when it wanted to celebrate, vicious when it wanted to scream about the decadence of power or inhumanity. The music was whatever anyone wanted it to be. And listeners bought it all.

The hippie as noble savage was firmly entrenched in the minds of young people as an attractive alternative to the things they had to put up with every day: school, petty jobs, lack of opportunity and restricted freedom. In the hippie, kids saw a model that could be imitated freely (after all, hippies were nothing if not free on either a full or part-time basis). One could buy some weird clothes, colored beads, scarves, earrings and what have you and check in or out any time. One did not have to run away to be free. Now it was possible to be a Weekend Hippie which, as the year came to a close, became a firmly established part of youth culture.

Only one word is needed to describe 1969: Woodstock. For three days in late August about a half-million people camped, ate, drank, slept and got high (among other things) on the excuse of listening to their favorite rock groups in the muddy fields of a farm in upstate New York. What emerged from that experience has been dubbed the

147

Woodstock Nation, so completely did the youth culture identify with the ideal it represented—an idylic realm of peace, love, brotherhood and rock music. Leading guitarist Jimi Hendrix provided its national anthem, playing an extraordinary, moving rendition of "The Star-Spangled Banner" (complete with bombs bursting in air), capturing all the pent-up sorrow and frustration of a nation turning upon itself. Woodstock was not a nation by any stretch of the imagination, but it was a symbol of sorts, a rally point at which young people everywhere could nod and say to those who gave them a bad time about their hair or music, "Look at Woodstock. That was beautiful."

In a sort of fanciful, myopic way, Woodstock *was* beautiful. In their lemminglike drive to believe in the dream of peace and love, the believers naively closed their eyes to the grossness of Woodstock. In many ways an artistic and financial flop (the $1.3 million lost by concert promoters to the festival was later more than recouped to the tune of $5 million a month when a smash-hit film and soundtrack were released), the unpleasant aspects of five hundred thousand people living on inadequate food, with inadequate toilet facilities, inadequate medical care and inadequate shelter, were completely overlooked. Woodstock was a symbolic triumph for the counterculture which proclaimed, "See, it really is true; we *can* live together in peace." The proclamation was at once a promise and a challenge. Sadly, it was a promise that could not be fulfilled, and a challenge that could not be ignored.

The next festival to take up the banner was Altamont. In December of 1969 the Rolling Stones had completed a nationwide tour and let it be known that they planned a free concert near San Francisco. Everyone was determined that this would be the biggest and best festival ever. Despite the fact that the festival site was switched

148

a mere twenty-four hours before starting time, an estimated three hundred thousand fans crowded the Altamont Speedway, a racetrack located some forty miles outside San Francisco.

Almost from the beginning death was in the air. Drugs circulated freely as the security guards, Hell's Angels bought for the event with the promise of $500 worth of beer, kept order with knives and pool cues. The festival turned into a disaster. The crushing weight of too many people, too many desires, too much self-indulgence and too little love pushed the once-glorious hippie dream to the breaking point. At Altamont the dream broke down; the bright day-glo colors ran, washed away by the reality of what the counterculture had become.

What it had become was horribly demonstrated as thousands of young people idly watched as one of their own, a young Black man, was brutally stabbed and beaten to death by Hell's Angels, while the band played on. Drugs claimed other lives that day, a total of four in all. And with them died the intimations of grandeur which the counterculture had so long espoused. The sweet dream of peace and love in the kingdom of flower children was shattered. In its place a cold reality set in: not peace but violence, not love but selfishness. Even the flowers turned out to be garbage. The end had come quickly. In less than four months since its triumph the promise had been broken.

The counterculture lingered in a state of shock after Altamont. Other megaconcerts were tried, but none ever achieved success. The soul had gone out of the movement. The magic was gone—*if* it had ever existed.

By 1970 popular music had arrived at what some have called its worst crisis. The hopes of an entire generation, so full and bright, had come to zero. Old favorites continued to be popular, to make and sell records. But the

149

music flailed the air looking for direction, some new sign to point the way. And as luck or chance would have it, the sign was going up, painted in large letters for all to see. Rock, which had nearly destroyed itself through its own violence and decadence, would package and sell just that: violence, sex and degeneration. Glitter rock had arrived.

While the Artful Degenerates were warming up in the wings, stage center was held by solo artists and soul groups. Actually, soul music had been thriving all along, but it was overshadowed somewhat by the more bombastic display of hard rock. Now, as the hard stuff ebbed, its strength sapped, its edge dulled, soul demonstrated it had life. Gladys Knight and the Pips, Aretha Franklin, a new group called the Jackson 5 and an old group called the Four Tops churned out a string of hits.

The Beatles, newly split into four solo acts, let loose some uneven live movie/concert tapes which made brief appearances on the charts. Crosby, Stills and Nash (later, Young) were the hot new group; their smooth, vocally rich country-rock style was the rage of the moment. All the while, glowering in the depths, monster rock was waiting. But for now, rock music enjoyed a year of grace.

When the monster arrived, it came in force in 1971 in the person of Alice Cooper. Actually, Alice was a group of unusually long-haired, freaky-looking gay rejects. They had been playing as a group for several years when their leader, a protestant minister's son named Vincent Furnier, changed his name to Alice Cooper, and the group began recording under that name. They were the first of the shock-rock storm troopers to take the stage. But others soon followed their lead, dreaming up nightmarish performances of their own. Groups like Black Sabbath and Grand Funk Railroad, and individuals like David Bowie kept the audiences guessing.

But monster rock did not dominate the marketplace.

The early seventies were also tempered with mellow offerings from stars such as Chicago and John Denver. Joni Mitchell and Jackson Browne came along to lend a completely novel quality to rock: understanding. Along with others, such as Paul Simon and Randy Newman, they represented the thoughtful artistic singer/songwriters who carefully articulate the present state of the human experience, sans smoke bombs and power chords.

Pop music, usually relegated to the lower echelons of gum-popping teenyboppers, started making inroads into the very sanctuary of hard-core rockaholics. The group that pulled this trick was a brother-sister team, well-scrubbed cherubs with no rough edges, the Carpenters. Reworking old Beatles material, soul favorites and a Coca-Cola ad, and using their own brand of multilayered vocal tracks featuring Karen Carpenter's honey voice, the Carpenters carved out a stronghold on the heights of Top 40 AM radio, rock's supreme bastion.

But the one group which perhaps best typifies the early seventies (although now nearly forgotten) was a quartet of backwoods rockers who called themselves Creedence Clearwater Revival. Their sound was pure gold, easily distinguishable from any other around—clean, countrified, simple melodies set to a basic, jumpy rock beat. No heavy artillery, no screaming guitars or gut-wrenching emotional displays, just straight-ahead, old-fashioned rock 'n' roll. Grassroots stuff. They professed no message, spiritual, political, social or otherwise. Yet from 1969 to 1972 they held all listeners in their sway.

That a group like that could become so popular says something about the state of rock at the time and what people were feeling. It was almost as if everyone was burned out from the overkill of the sixties. The musicians

151

who rose to minister to the high-decible deafened legion were quieter, less-complicated sorts. The early seventies saw the beginnings of most artists which continue their careers today, changing little from their inception.

In a way, that's the story of the seventies, middle and end. The seventies can be seen as a musical smorgasbord, a little of everything, but not too much of any one thing. There may be more to choose from in the way of musical style now—everything from Gay Rock to God Rock—but the excessively high price tag attached to any commercial venture in the music field almost guarantees that there will be less and less to go around. Those who have been able to capture our ears are those with staying power, not perhaps the most dynamic but the most tenacious. The rock decade closed out much as it started, with little in between to distinguish itself from one year to another. There have been supergroups, superstars and super-sounds (everything in the seventies was super), but not one genuine galvanizing moment.

The audiences, less activistic and militant, were quite docile and introspective. If a label is to be pasted on the seventies, it is surely "Me." The music reflects this. The audience is able to support the smorgasbord of superstars because it is too preoccupied with itself to become unified under any one personality or group for any length of time. Performers talk less about the crowd and more about the individuals in the audience. The Rebel Generation of the sixties gave way to the Me Generation of the seventies. What the eighties hold in store remains to be seen, but most assuredly there will be rock music. For as long as young people feel repressed and awkward, as long as society can indulge one affluent and self-centered genera-tion after another, as long as there is electricity, there will be rock music. Rock is here to stay.

Notes

Chapter 3

[1]Jonathan Eisen, *The Age of Rock* (New York: Random House, Vintage Books, 1969), p. 126.

[2]Tony Palmer, *All You Need is Love: The Story of Popular Music* (New York: Penguin, 1976), p. 217.

[3]Ibid.

[4]"G-Man Blues: Elvis Wanted to Help," *Time,* 24 July 1978, p. 23.

[5]"Dennis Benson, Chaplain to the Stars," *With,* February 1979, p. 13.

Chapter 4

[1]Bob Larson, *The Day Music Died* (Carol Stream, Ill.: Creation House, 1972), pp. 87-88.

[2]Palmer, p. 7.

[3]Ibid., pp. 5-6.

[4]Bruno Nettl, *Music in Primitive Culture* (Cambridge, Mass.: Harvard University Press, 1956), p. 128.

Chapter 5

[1]Kate Hevener, "The Affective Character of Major and Minor Modes in Music," *American Journal of Psychology* 47 (1935): 103-18.

[2]Larson, p. 111.

[3]William S. Kroger and William D. Fezel, *Hypnosis and Behavior Modification* (Philadelphia: J. B. Lippincott, 1976), p. 291.

[4]Larson, p. 120.

[5]"Can Rock 'n' Roll Lead to Rack 'n' Ruin?" *Los Angeles Times,* 5 February 1978.

Chapter 6

[1]Ian Whitcomb, *After the Ball* (New York: Simon and Schuster, 1972), p. 202.
[2]John Rublowsky, *Popular Music* (New York: Basic Books, 1971), p. 95.
[3]Whitcomb, p. 202.
[4]Kip Kirby, "Country Lyrics Reflecting 1980s Social Permissiveness," *Billboard,* 11 October 1980, p. 1.
[5]Ibid., p. 32.
[6]Ibid.
[7]Jane Stuart Smith and Betty Carlson, *A Gift of Music* (Westchester, Ill.: Good News Publishers, 1978), p. 128.

Chapter 7

[1]J. G. Machen, *Christianity and Culture* (Huemoz, Switzerland: L'Abri Fellowship, 1969), p. 4.
[2]Thurlow Spurr, "Gospel Music: Alive and Well," *Charisma,* July-August 1978, p. 46.

Chapter 8

[1]Richard Stanislaw, "Should We Rock the Boat over Rock Music?" *Eternity,* March 1977, p. 25.

Chapter 9

[1]Paul Johnson quoted in "Gospel Music," p. 46.
[2]M. Goldbeck in Erik Routley, *Twentieth Century Church Music* (New York: Oxford University Press, 1964), p. 114.
[3]Charles Etherington, *Protestant Worship Music* (New York: Holt, Rinehart and Winston, 1962), pp. 3-4.
[4]Jimmy Swaggart, "Contemporary Music," *The Evangelist,* July 1980, p. 3.
[5]Cyril Barnes, *God's Army,* p. 100.

Chapter 10

[1]Francis Schaeffer, *Art and the Bible* (Downers Grove: InterVarsity Press, 1973).
[2]Jimmy Swaggart, "Contemporary Music," p. 4.

Appendix

[1]Mike Jahn, *Rock* (New York: Quadrangle, The New York Times Book Co., 1973), p. 154.
[2]Jim Miller, ed., *The Rolling Stone Illustrated History of Rock and Roll* (New York: Random House, Rolling Stone Press, 1976), p. 174.
[3]William Shafer, *Rock Music* (Minneapolis: Augsburg, 1972), p. 56.

Bibliography

Barnes, Cyril. *God's Army*. Elgin, Ill.: David C. Cook, 1978.

Belz, Carl. *The Story of Rock, Second Edition*. New York: Harper and Row, Harper Colophon Books, 1972.

Cone, James H. *The Spirituals and the Blues*. New York: The Seabury Press, 1972.

Denisoff, R. Serge. *Solid Gold, The Popular Record Industry*. New Brunswick, N.J.: Transaction Books, 1975.

Eisen, Jonathan. *The Age of Rock*. New York: Random House, Vintage Books, 1969.

Etherington, Charles L. *Protestant Worship Music; It's History and Practice*. New York: Holt, Rinehart and Winston, 1962.

Gaston, E. Thayer. *Music in Therapy*. New York: Macmillan, 1968.

Grossman, Lloyd. *A Social History of Rock Music from the Greasers to Glitter Rock*. New York: David McKay, 1976.

Jahn, Mike. *Rock: From Elvis Presley to the Rolling Stones*. New York: Quadrangle, The New York Times Book Co., 1973.

Kroger, William S. and William D. Fezler. *Hypnosis and Behavior Modification: Imagery Conditioning*. Philadelphia: J. B. Lippincott, 1976.

Larson, Bob. *The Day Music Died*. Carol Stream, Ill.: Creation House, 1972.

──────────. *Rock*. Wheaton, Ill.: Tyndale, 1980.

──────────. *Rock and the Church*. Carol Stream, Ill.: Creation House, 1971.

Lundin, Robert W. *An Objective Psychology of Music*. 2nd ed. New York: The Ronald Press, 1967.

Machen, J. G. *Christianity and Culture*. Huemoz, Switzerland: L'Abri Fellowship, 1969.

McKinley, Edward H. *Marching to Glory*. New York: Harper and Row, 1980.

McLaughlin, Terence. *Music and Communication*. New York: St. Martin's, 1970.

Miller, Jim, ed. *The Rolling Stone Illustrated History of Rock and Roll*. New York: Random House, Rolling Stone Press, 1976.

Myra, Harold and Dean Merrill. *Rock, Bach and Superschlock.* Nashville: A. J. Holman Company, 1972.
Nanry, Charles, ed. *American Music from Storyville to Woodstock.* New Brunswick: N.J.: Transaction Books, 1972.
Nettl, Bruno. *Music in Primitive Culture.* Cambridge, Mass.: Harvard University Press, 1956.
Nite, Norm N. *Rock On, Volume II.* New York: Thomas Y. Crowell, 1978.
Palmer, Tony. *All You Need Is Love: The Story of Popular Music.* New York: Penguin Books, 1976.
Powell, Marvin. *The Psychology of Adolescence, Second Edition.* Indianapolis: Bobbs-Merrill, 1971.
Routley, Erik. *Twentieth Century Church Music.* New York: Oxford University Press, 1964.
_____. *Words, Music and the Church.* New York: Abingdon, 1968.
Rublowsky, John. *Black Music in America.* New York: Basic Books, 1971.
_____. *Popular Music.* New York: Basic Books, 1967.
Russell, Tony. *Black, Whites and Blues.* New York: Stein and Day, 1970.
Schaeffer, Francis A. *Art and the Bible.* Downers Grove, Ill.: Inter-Varsity Press, 1973.
Schafer, William. *Rock Music –Where It's Been, What It Means, Where It's Going.* Minneapolis: Augsburg, 1972.
Schimel, John L., M.D. *The Parent's Handbook on Adolescence.* New York: World, 1969.
Sesonske, Alexander, ed. *What is Art?* New York: Oxford University Press, 1965.
Smith, Jane Stuart and Betty Carlson. *A Gift of Music: Great Composers and Their Influence.* Westchester, Ill.: Good News Publishers, 1978.
Topp, Dale. *Music in the Christian Community.* Grand Rapids, Mich.: Eerdmans, 1976.
Vorath, Harry H. and Larry K. Brendtro. *Positive Peer Culture.* Chicago: Aldine, 1974.
Whitcomb, Ian. *After the Ball.* New York: Simon and Schuster, 1972.
Whittenburg, Rudolph M. *The Troubled Generation.* New York: Association Press, 1967.
Wolterstorff, Nicholas. *Art in Action.* Grand Rapids, Mich.: Eerdmans, 1980.